Lacy Sunsh

MW01195205

All About Rory The Sweet Urchin

Coloring Book Volume 12

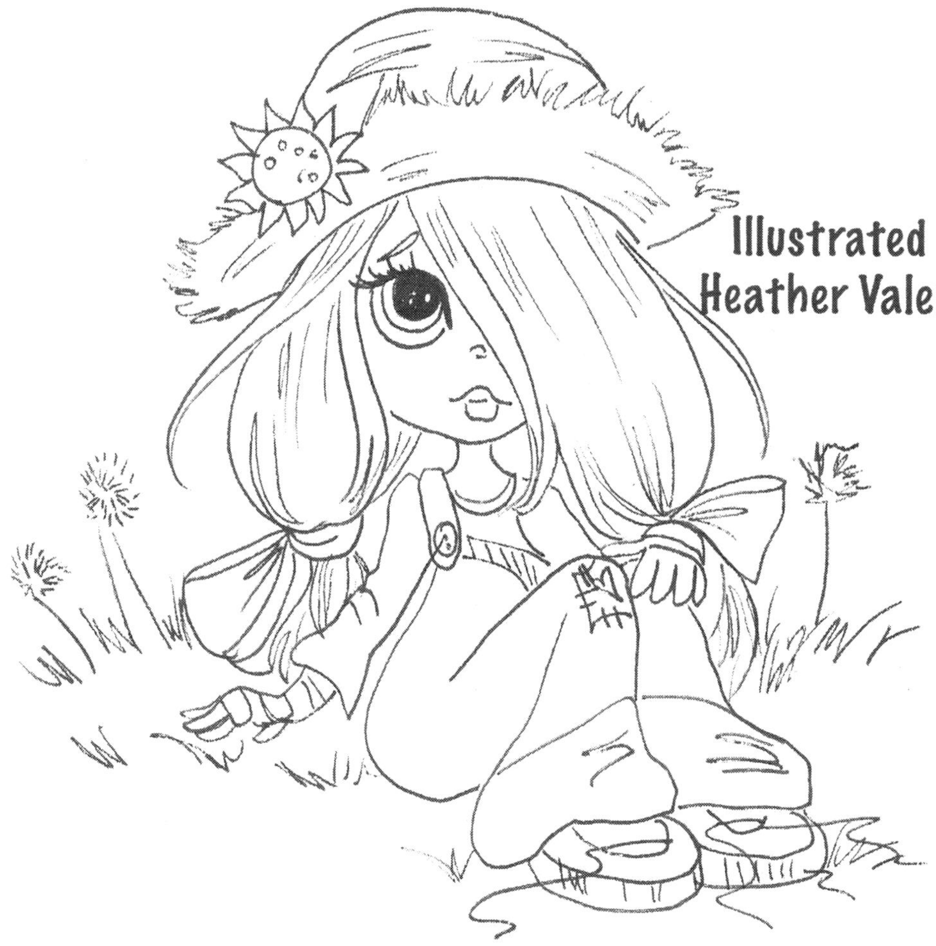

Illustrated By
Heather Valentin

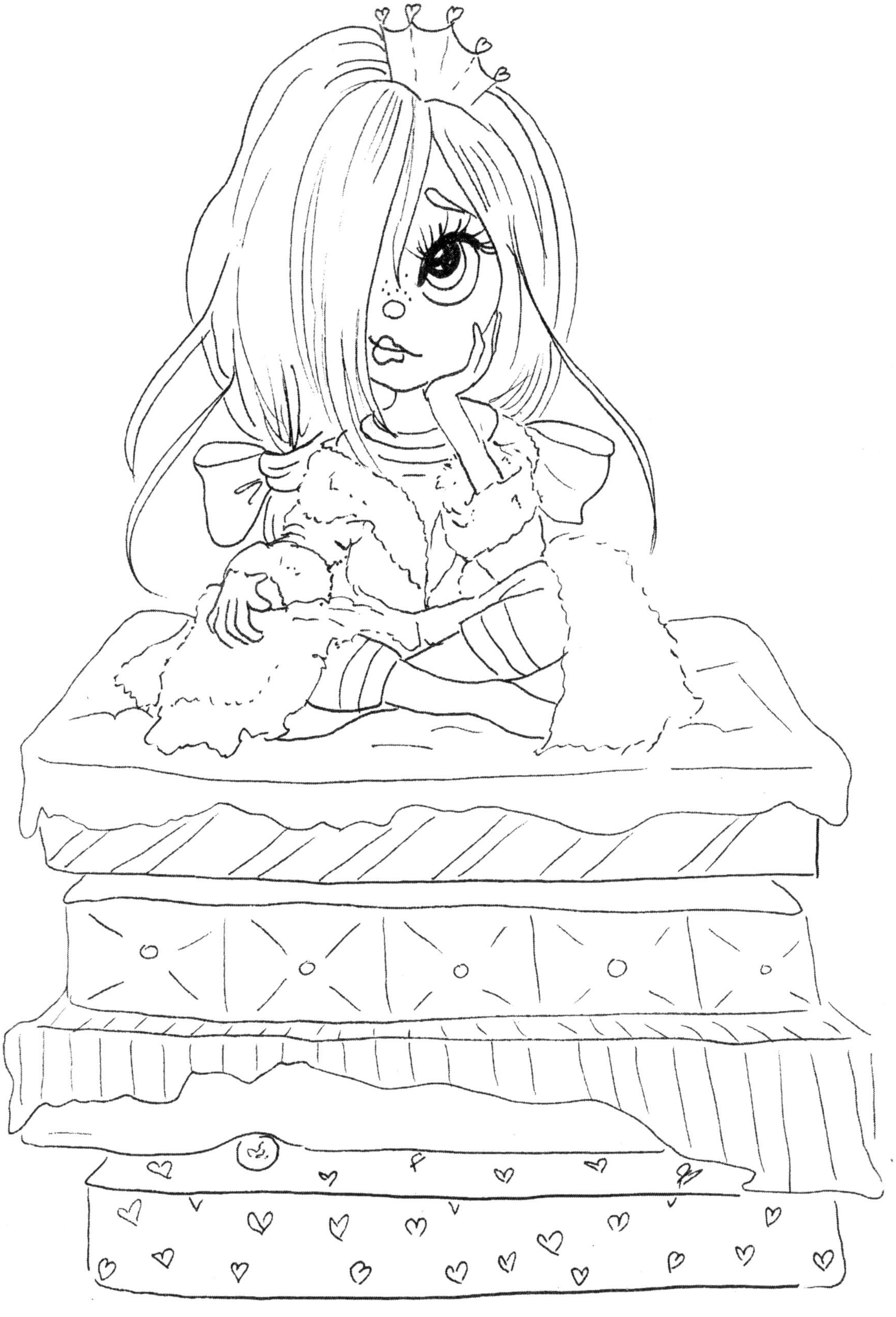

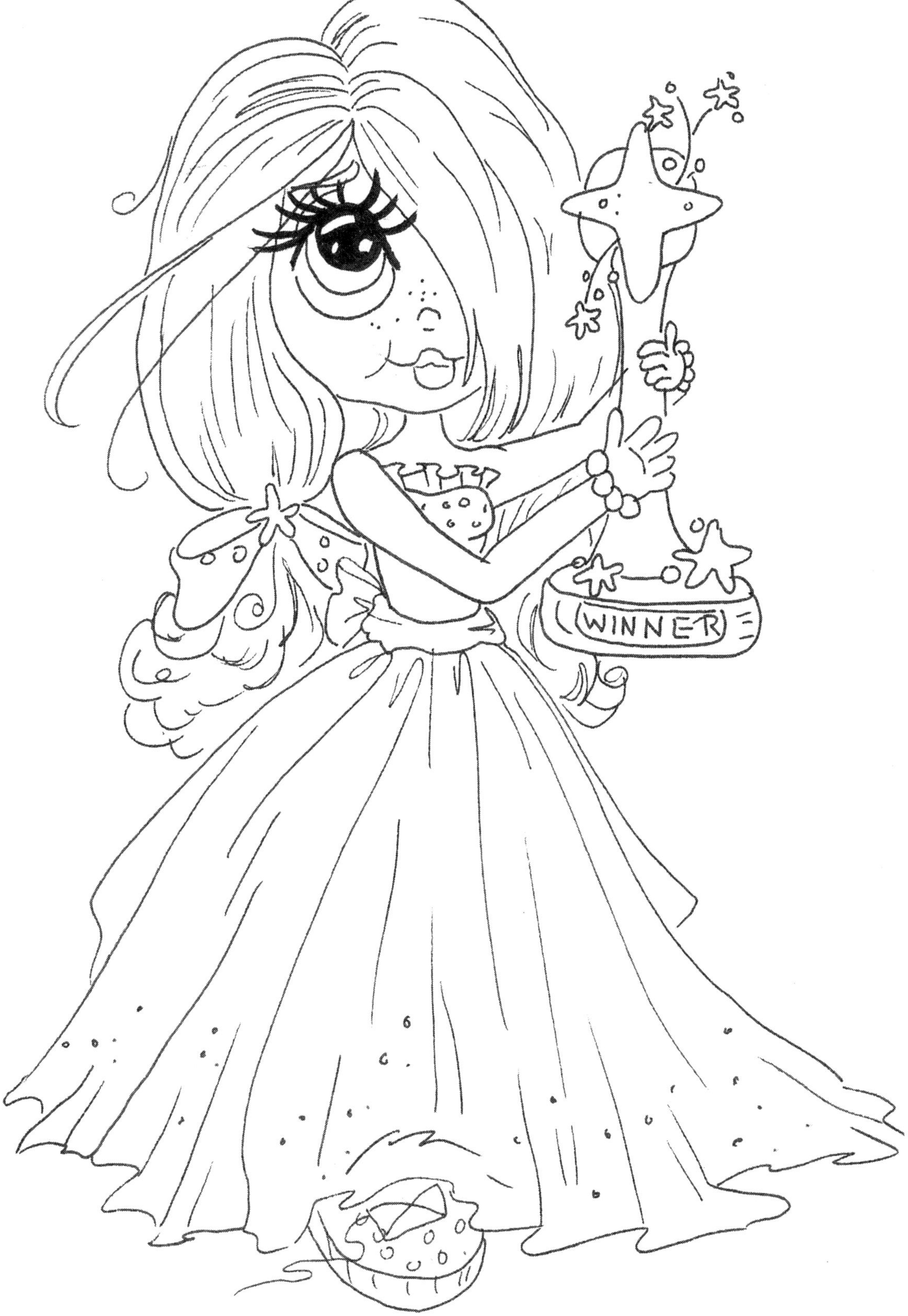
WINNER

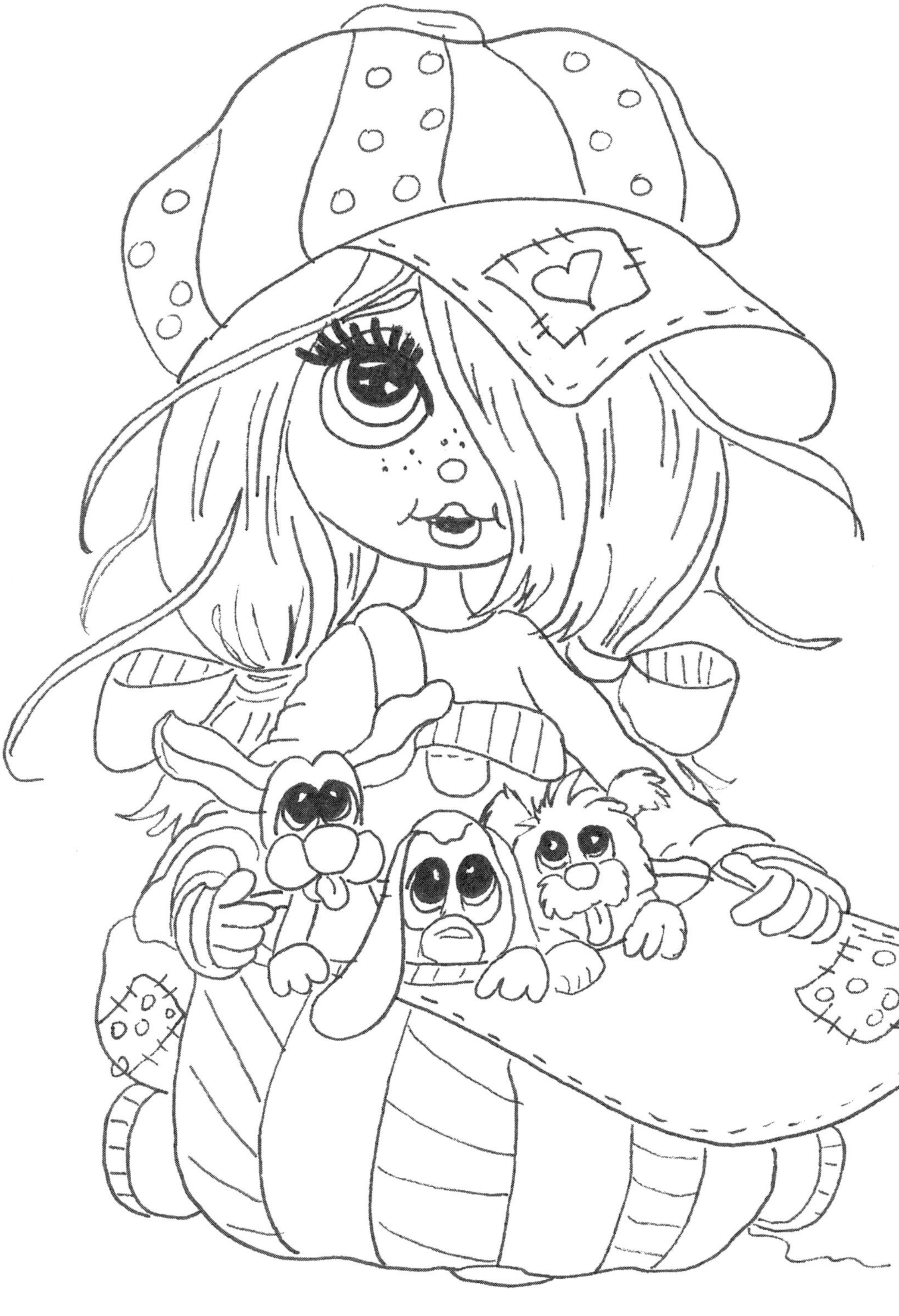

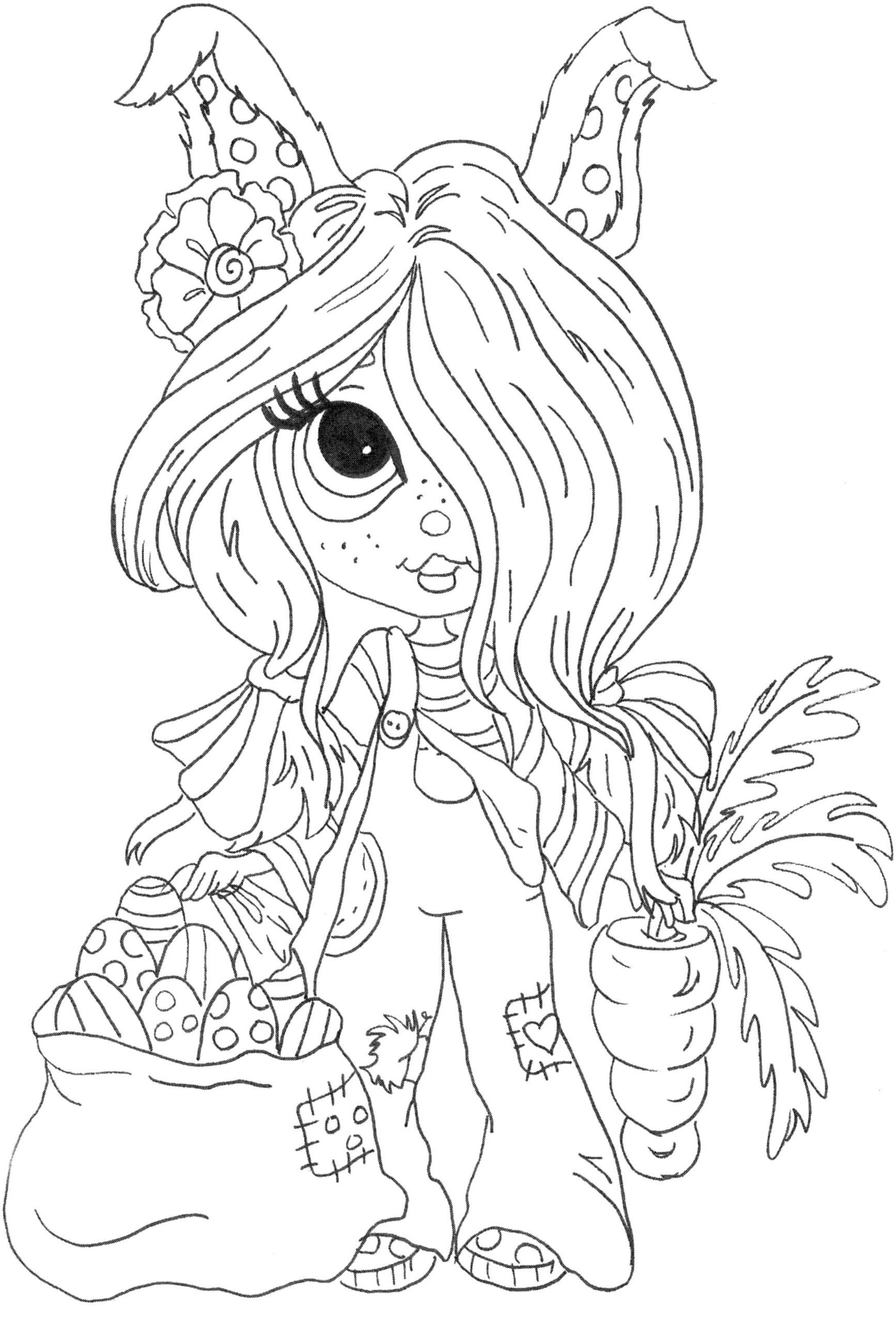

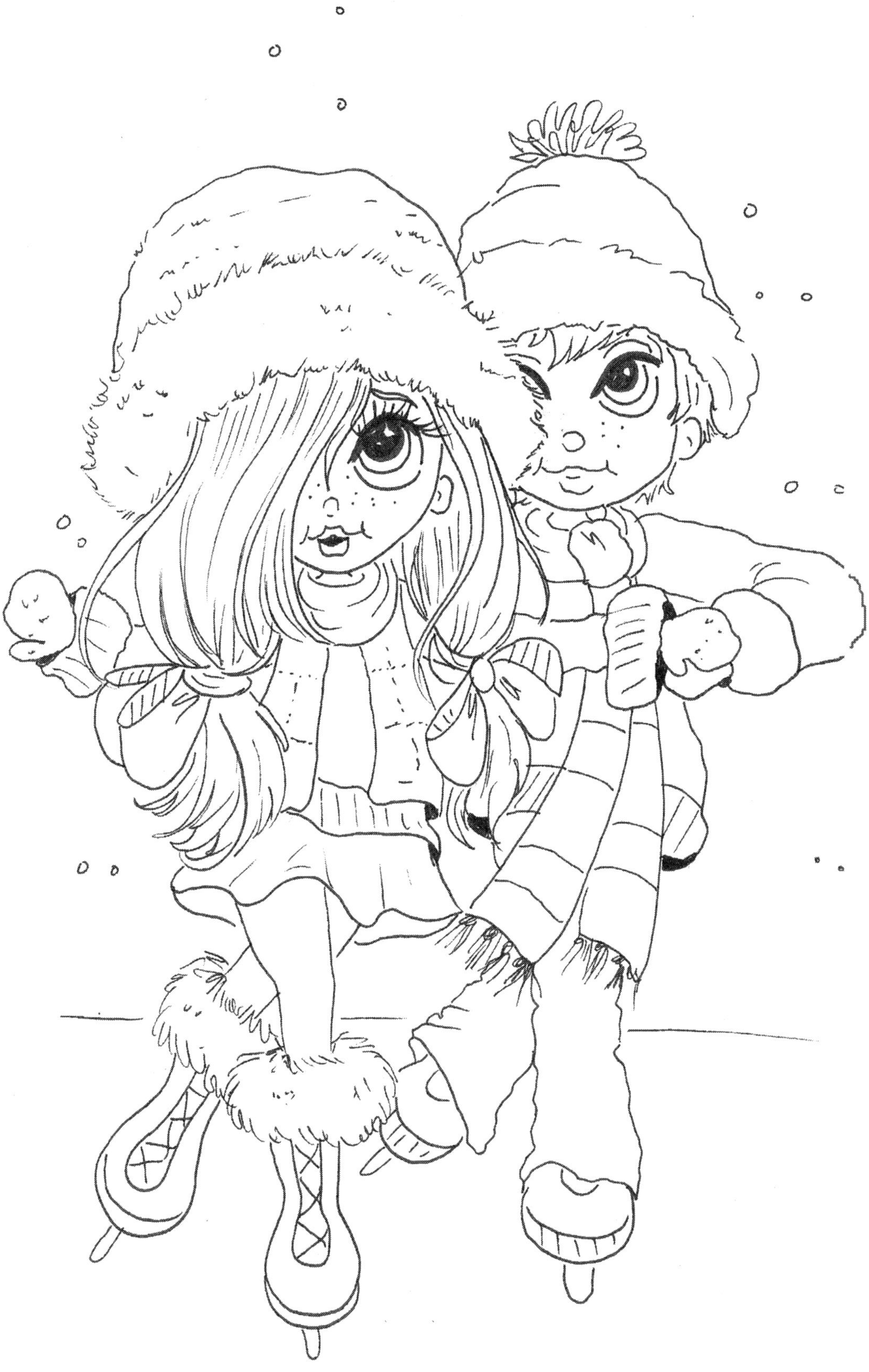

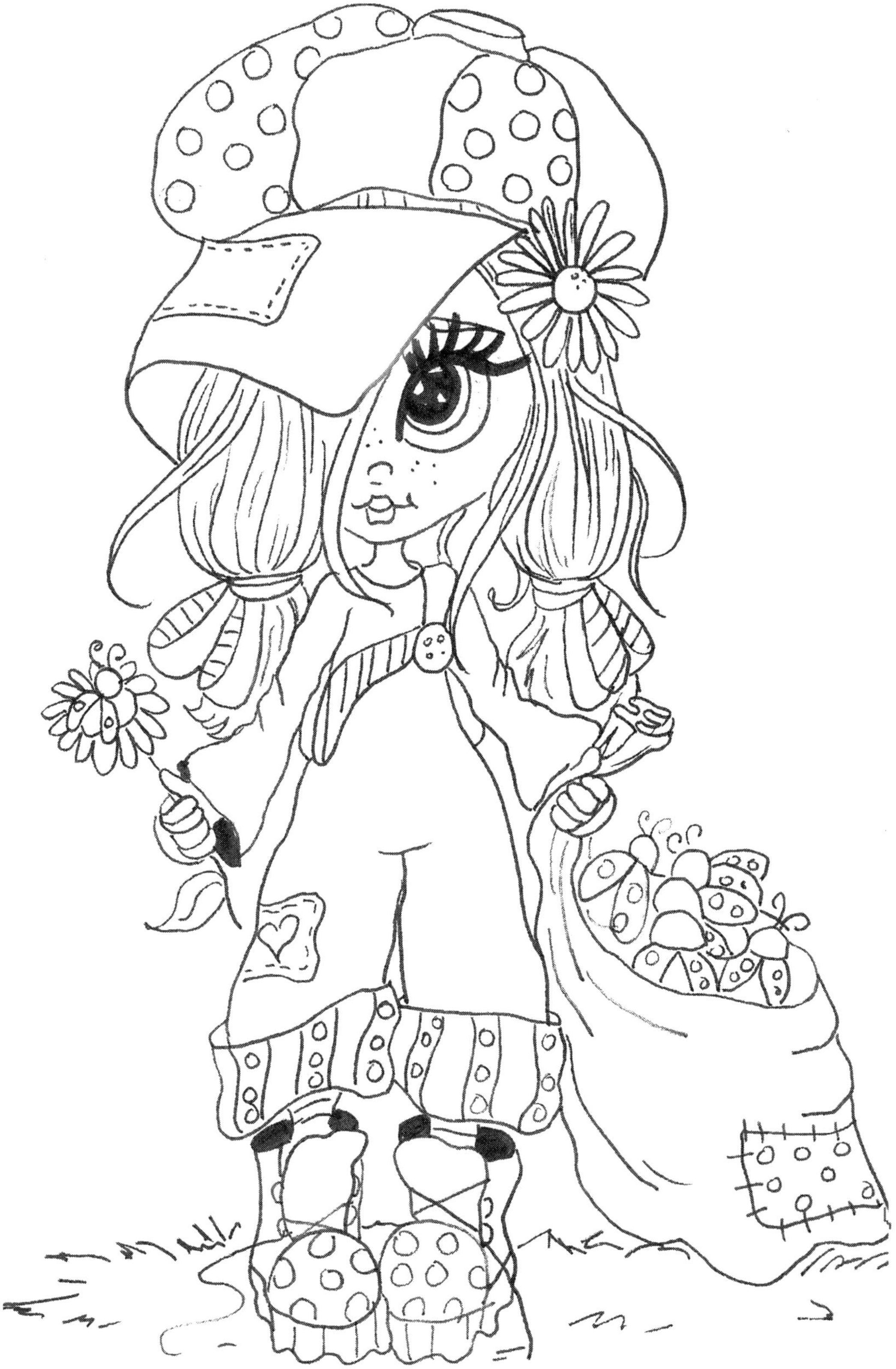

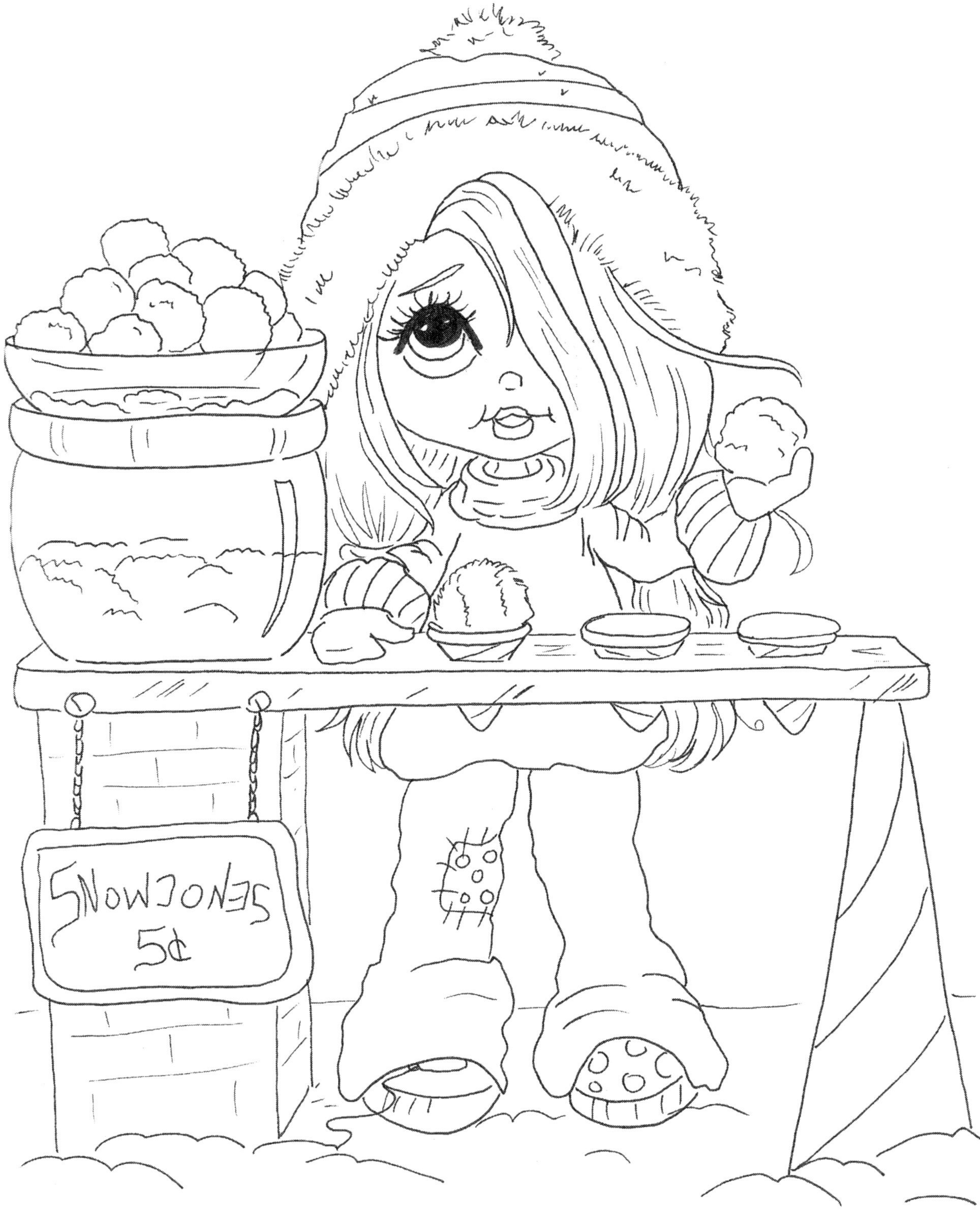
SNOWCONES
5¢

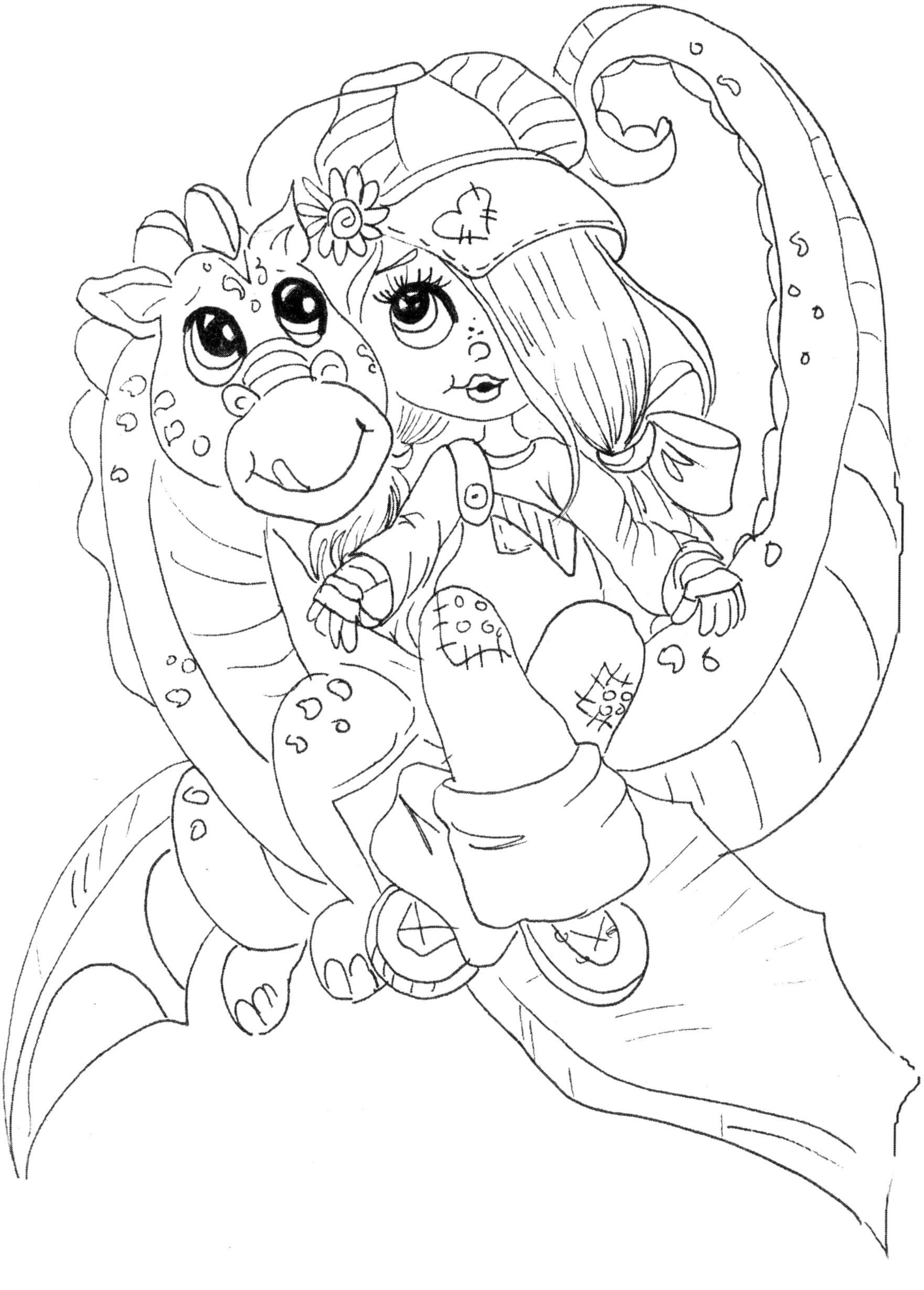

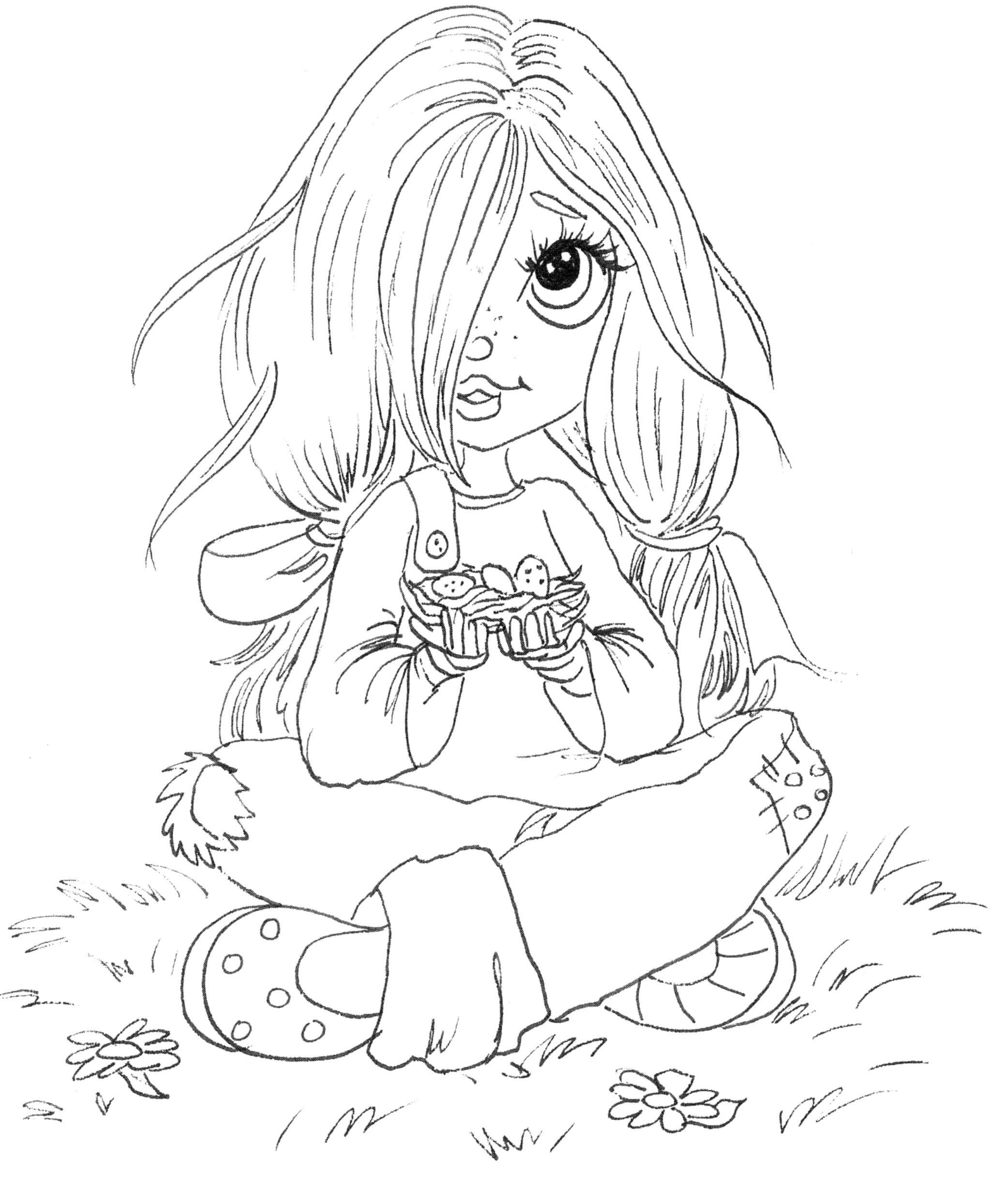

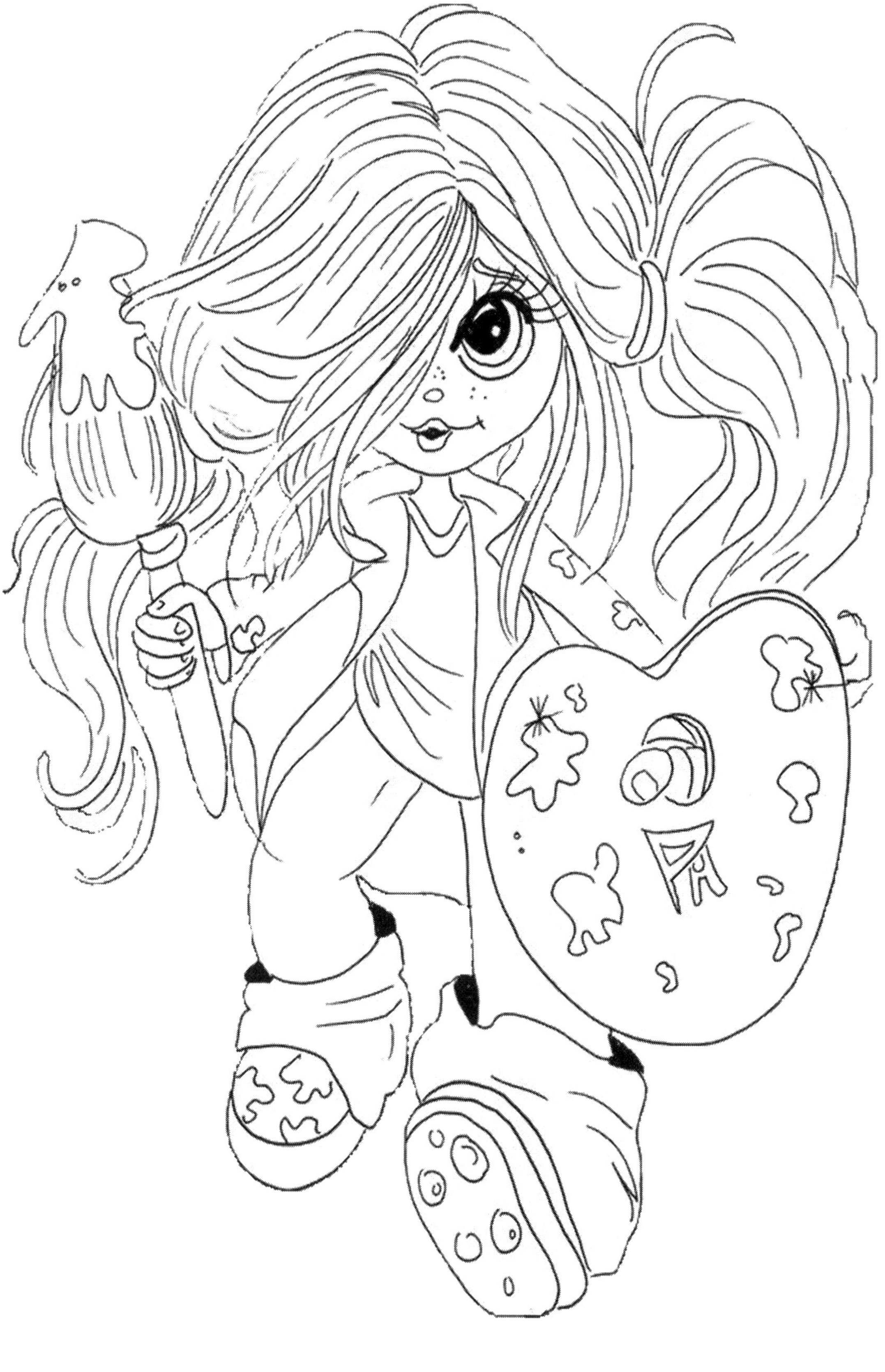

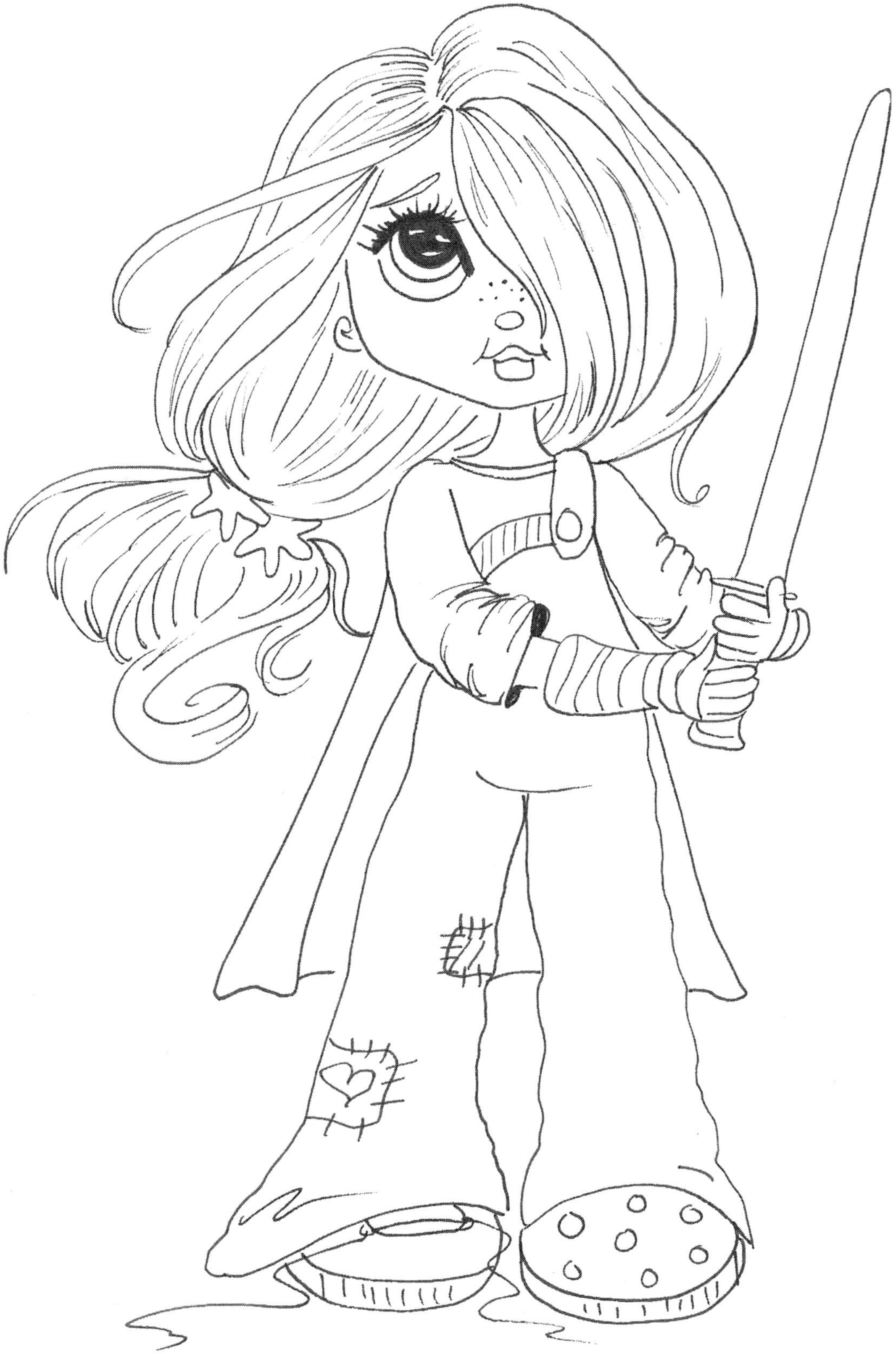

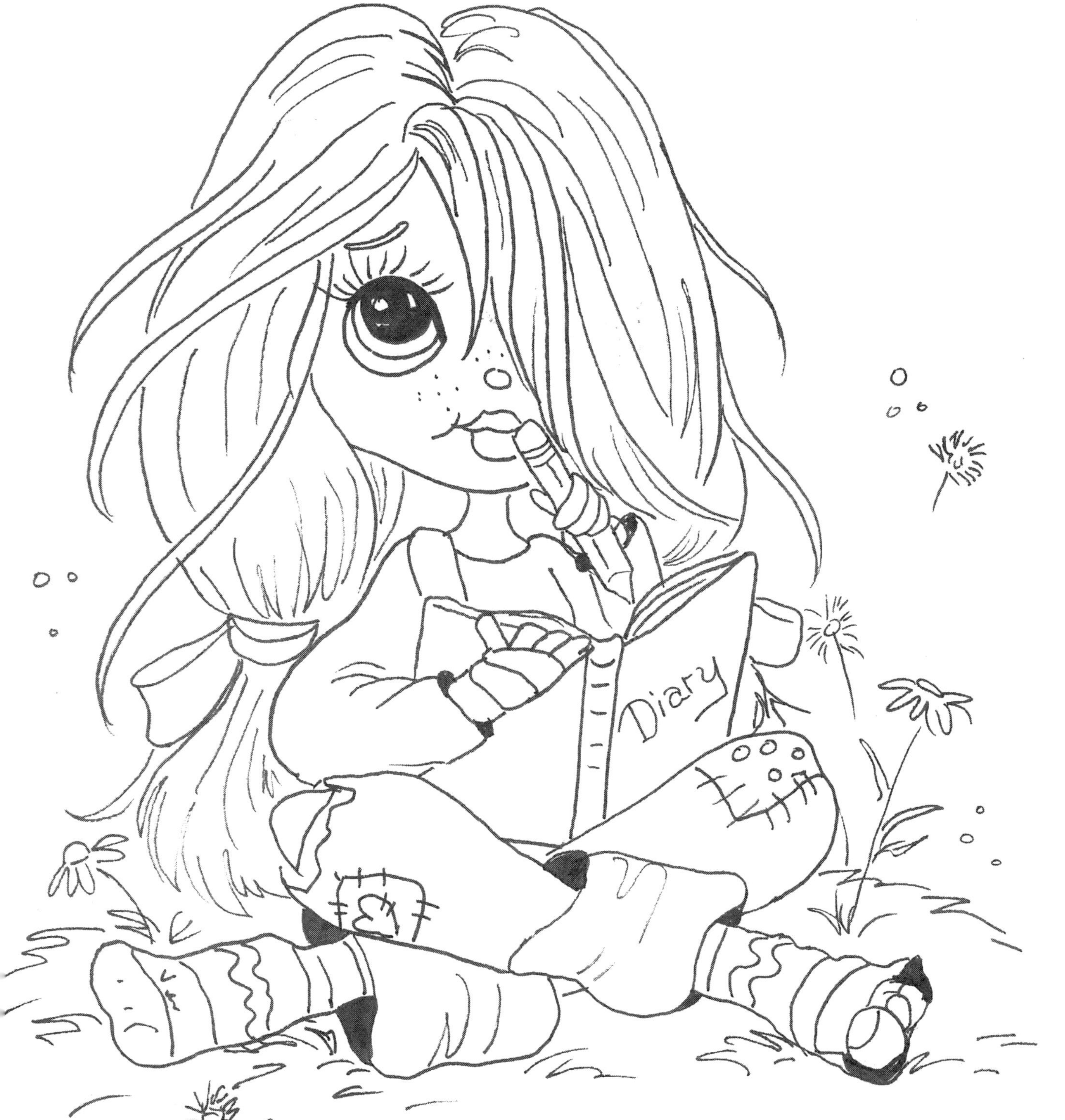
Diary

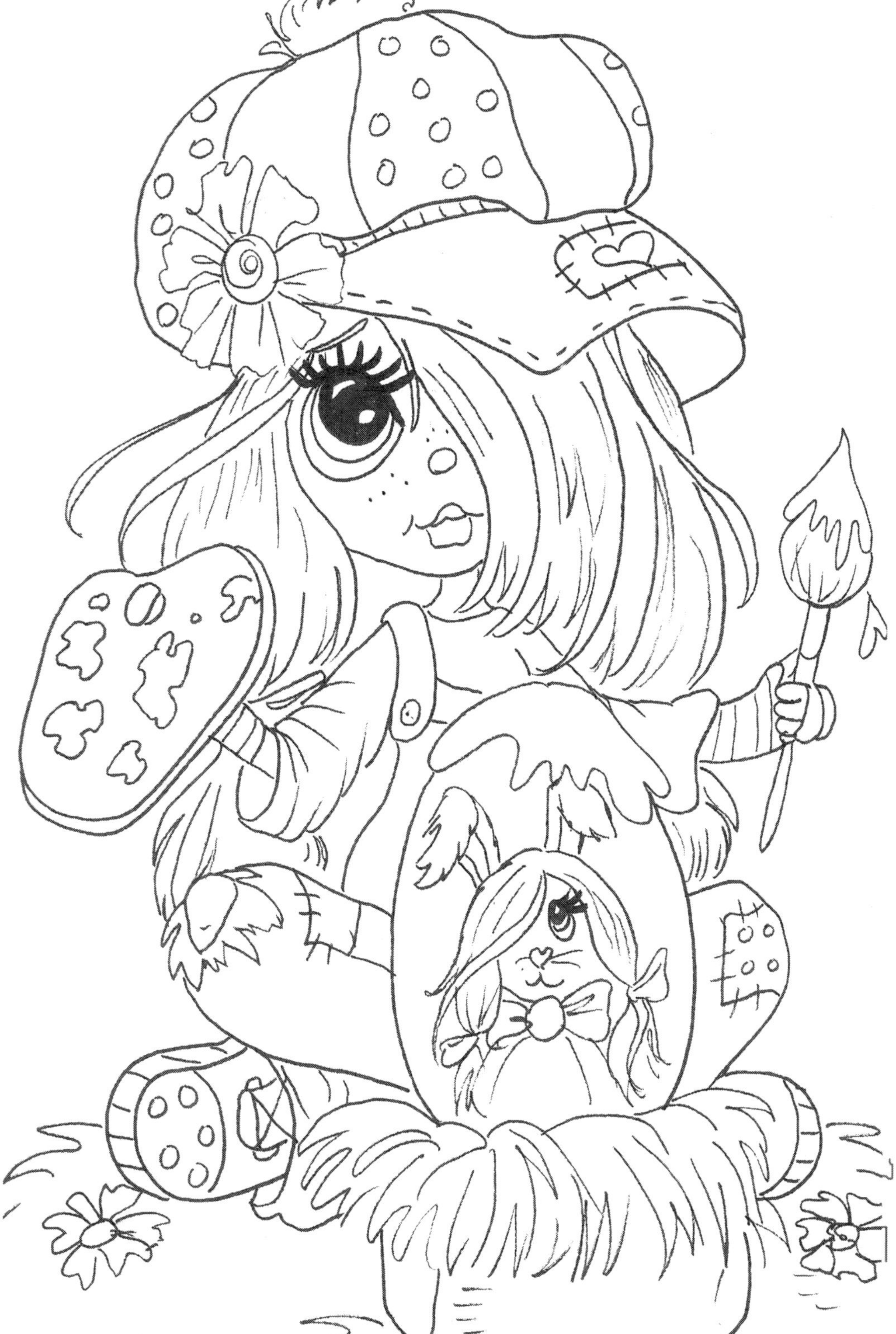

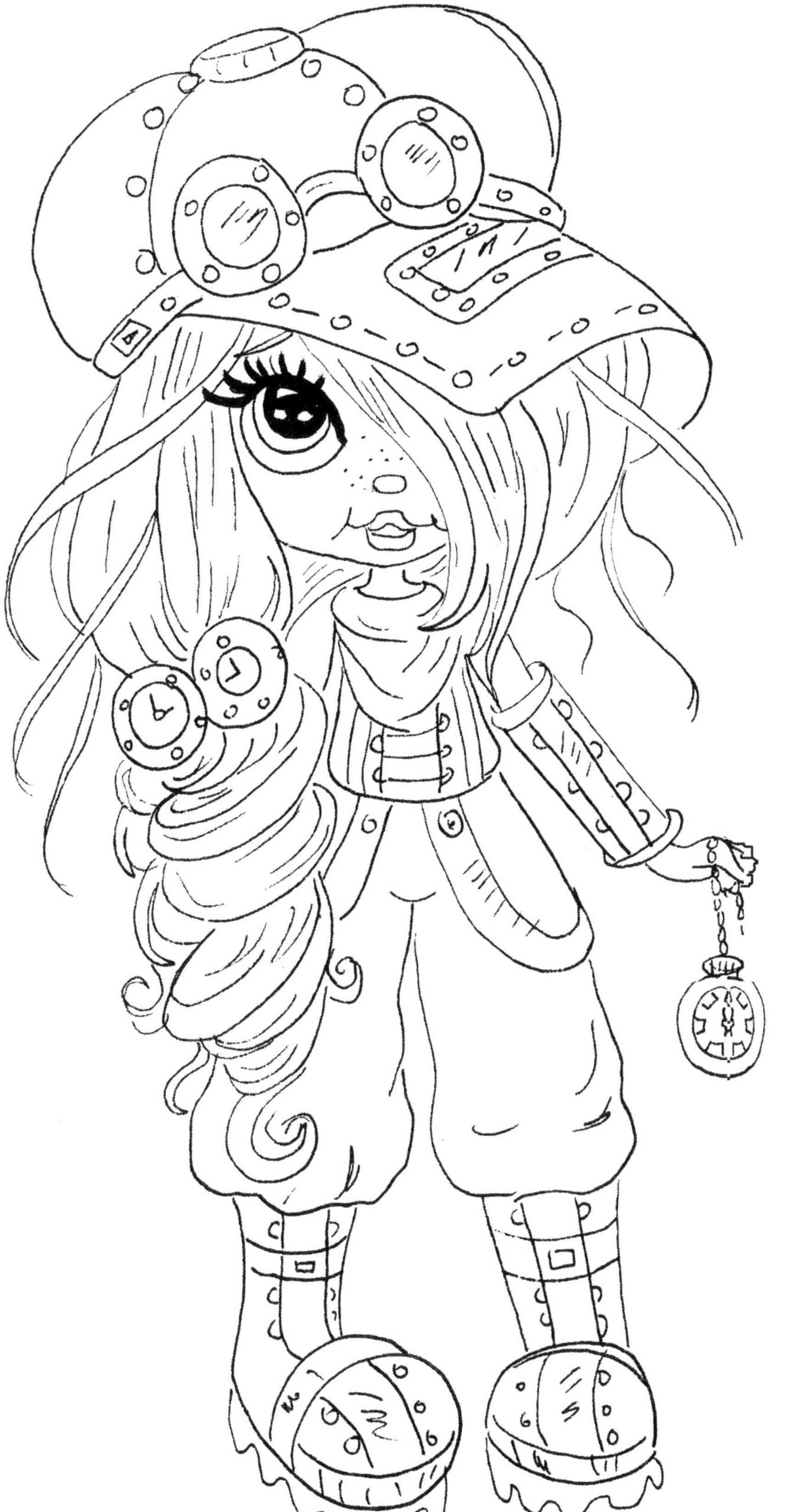

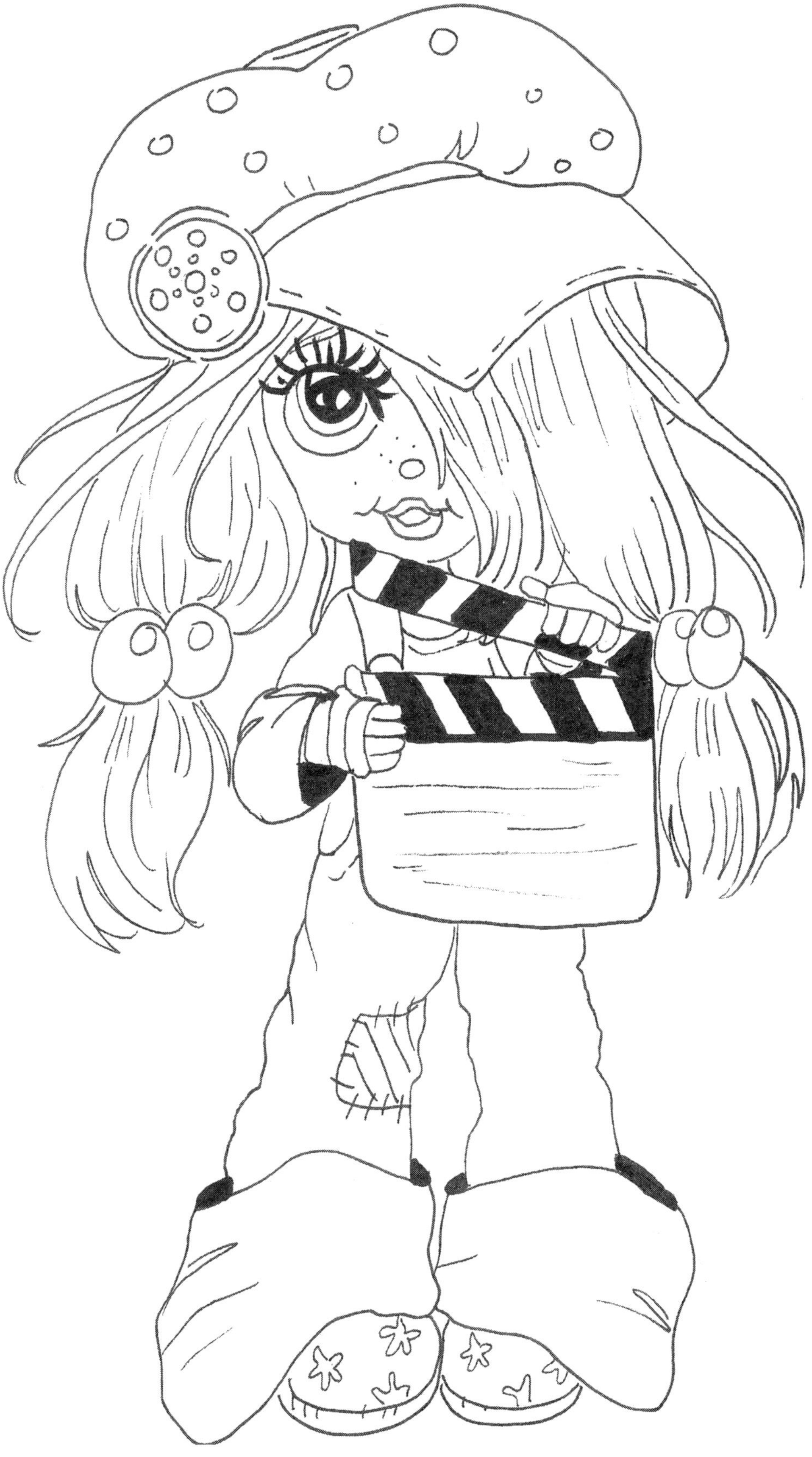

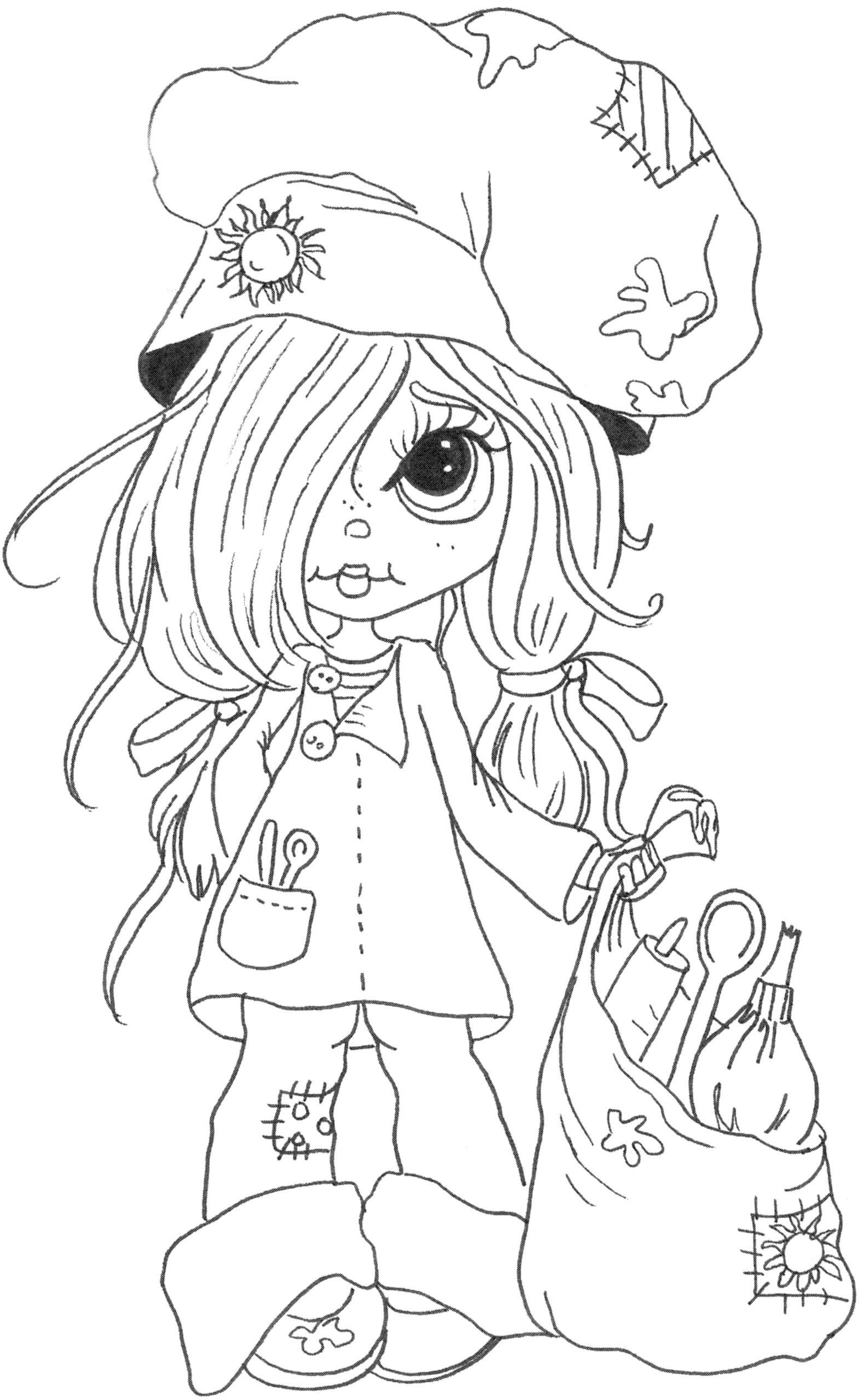

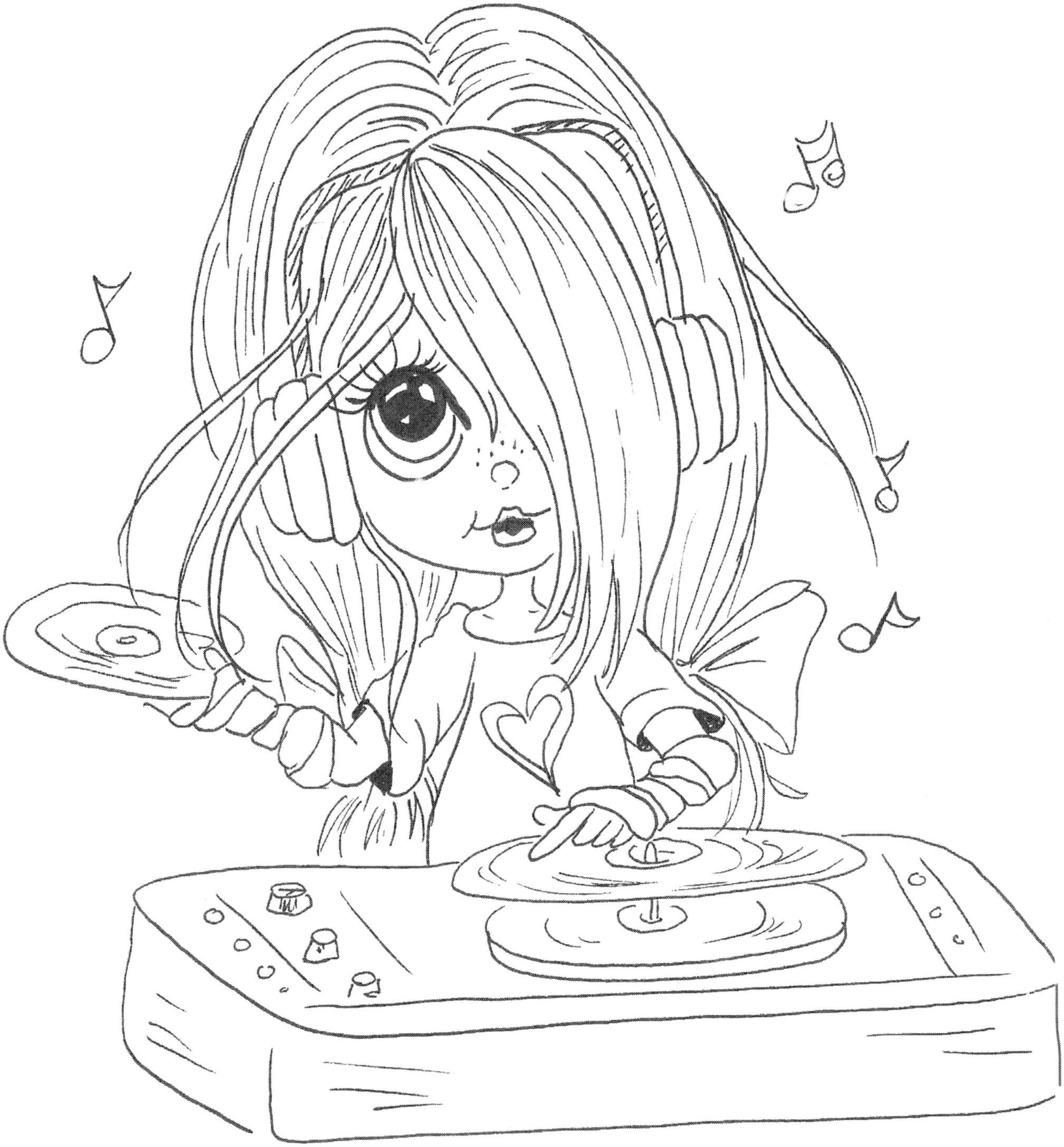

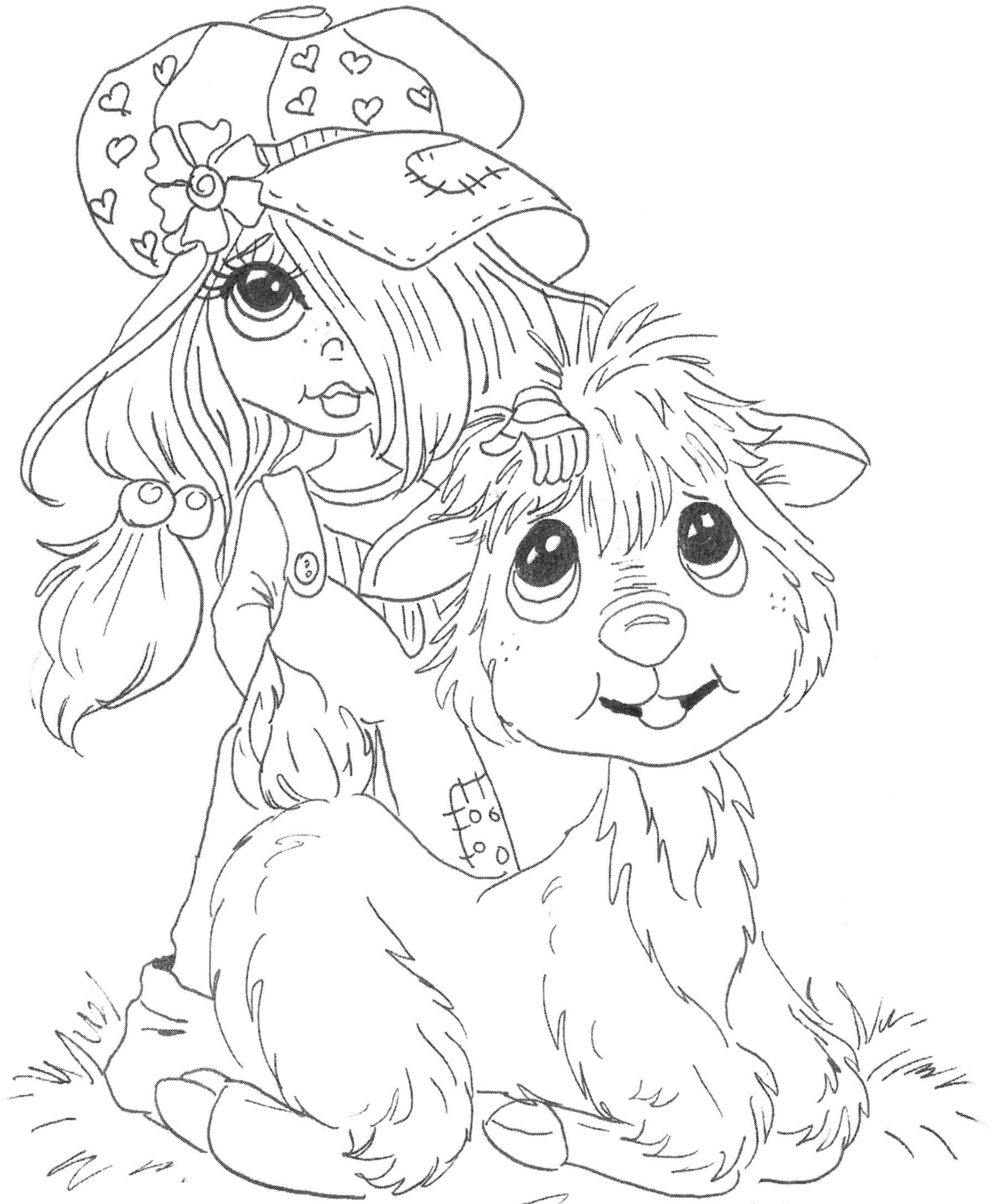

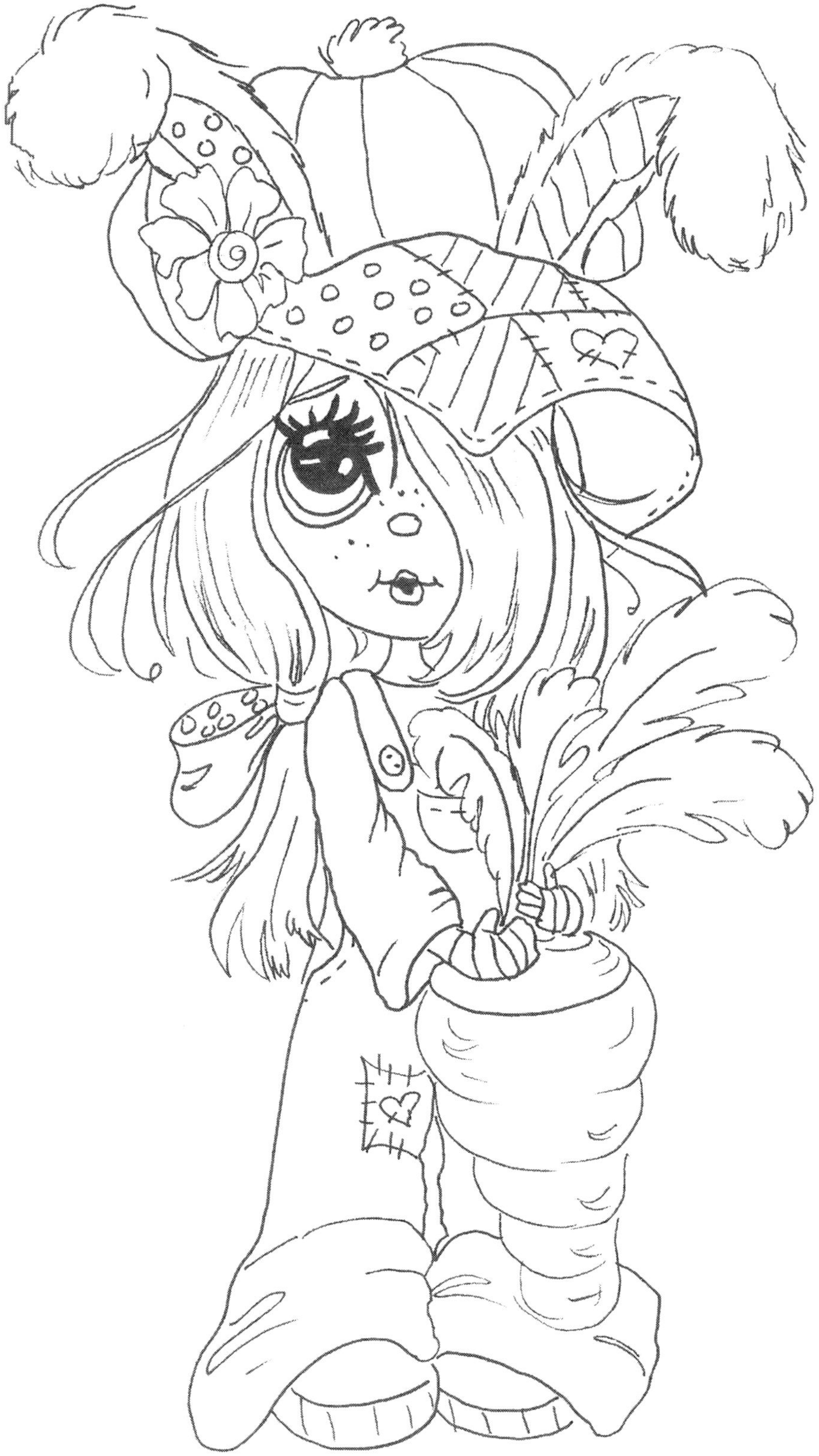

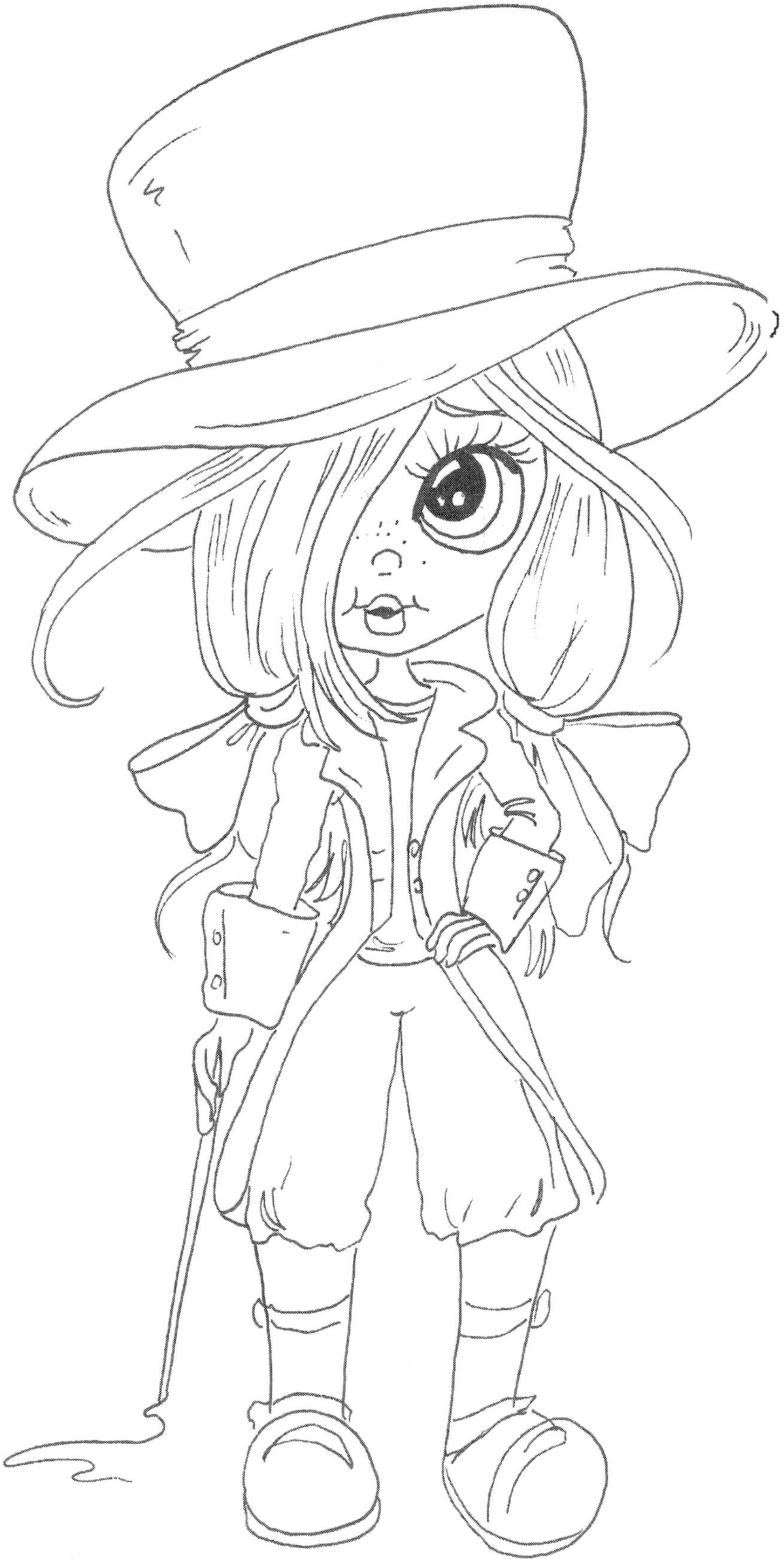

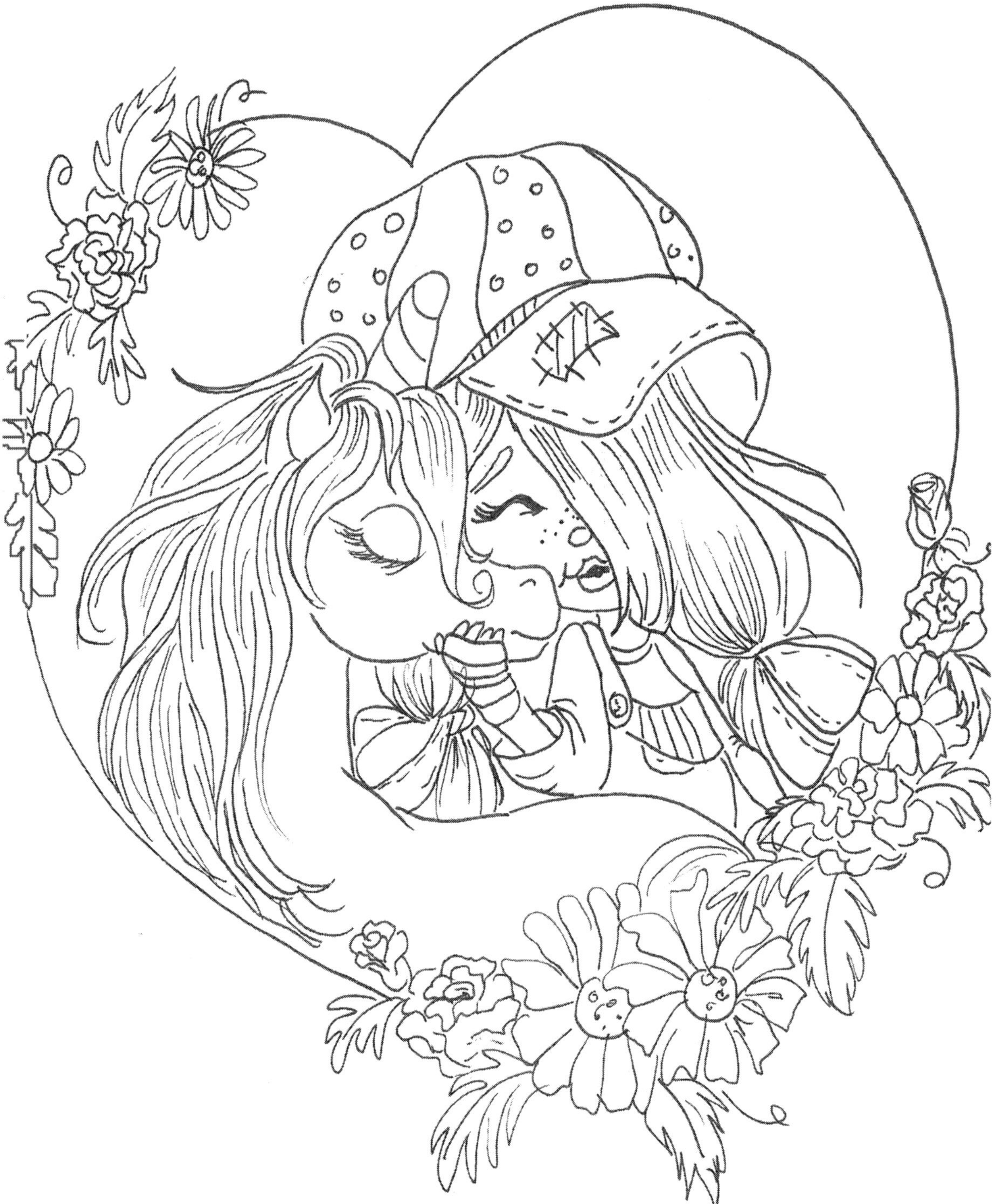

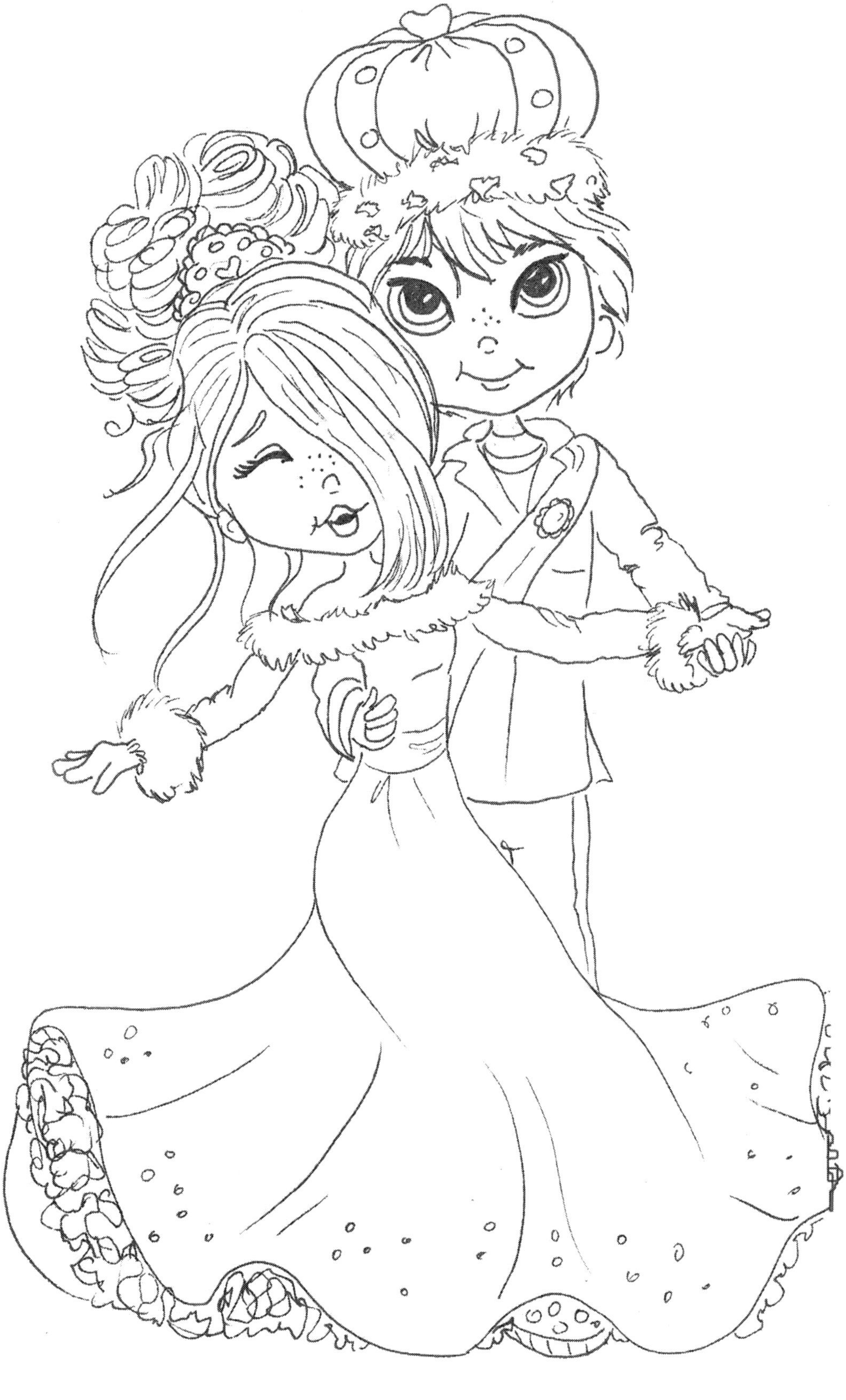

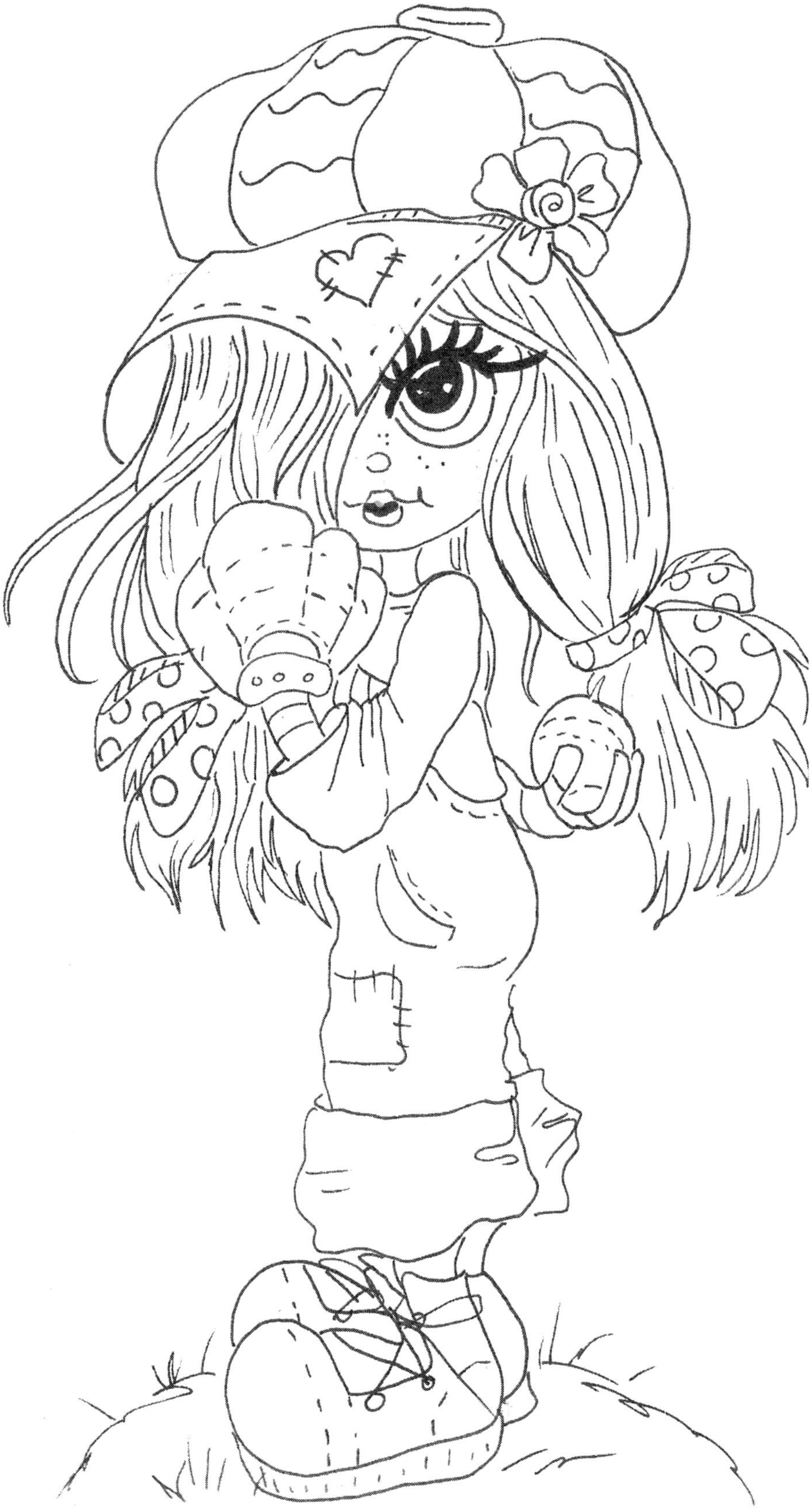

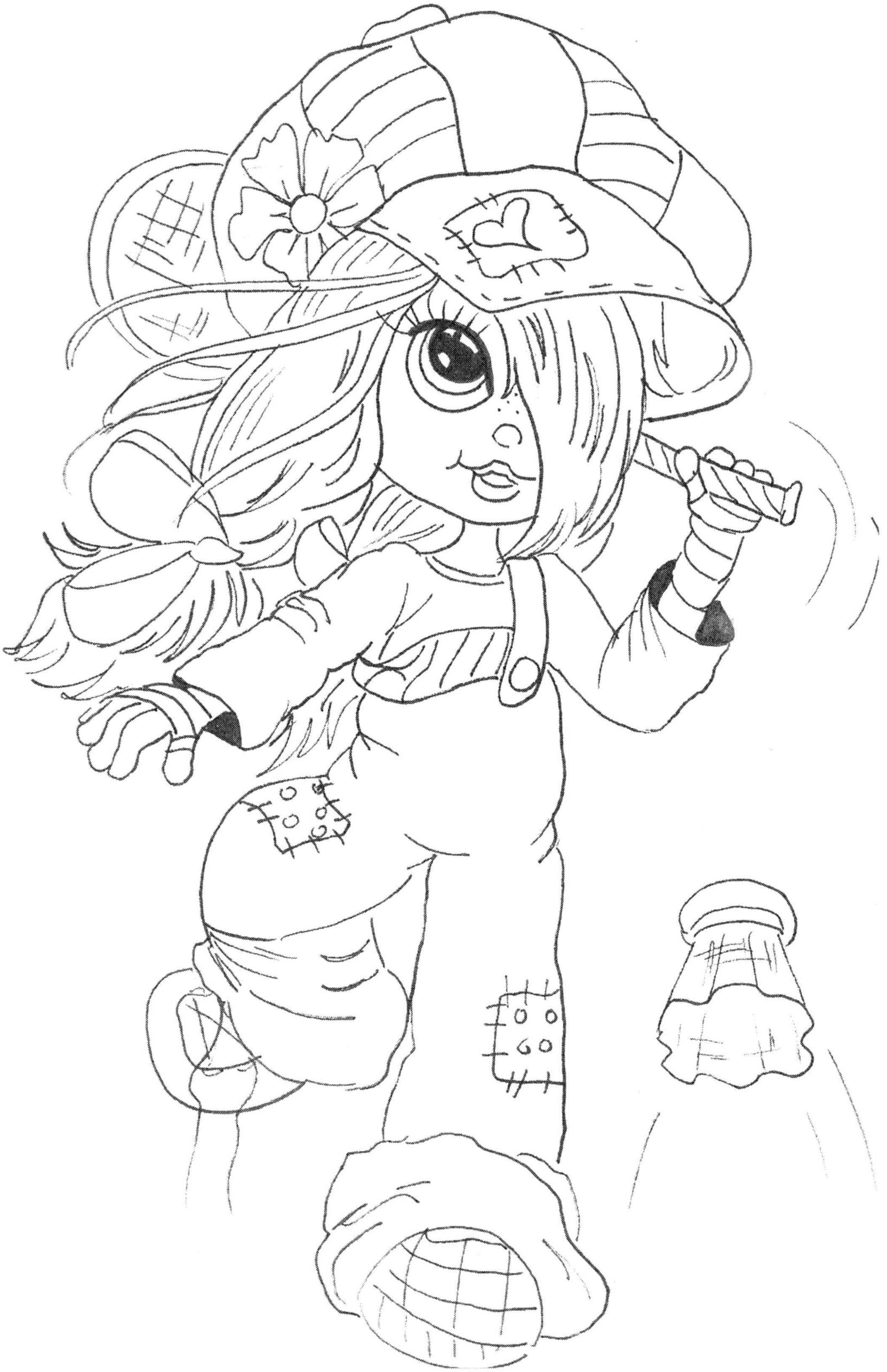

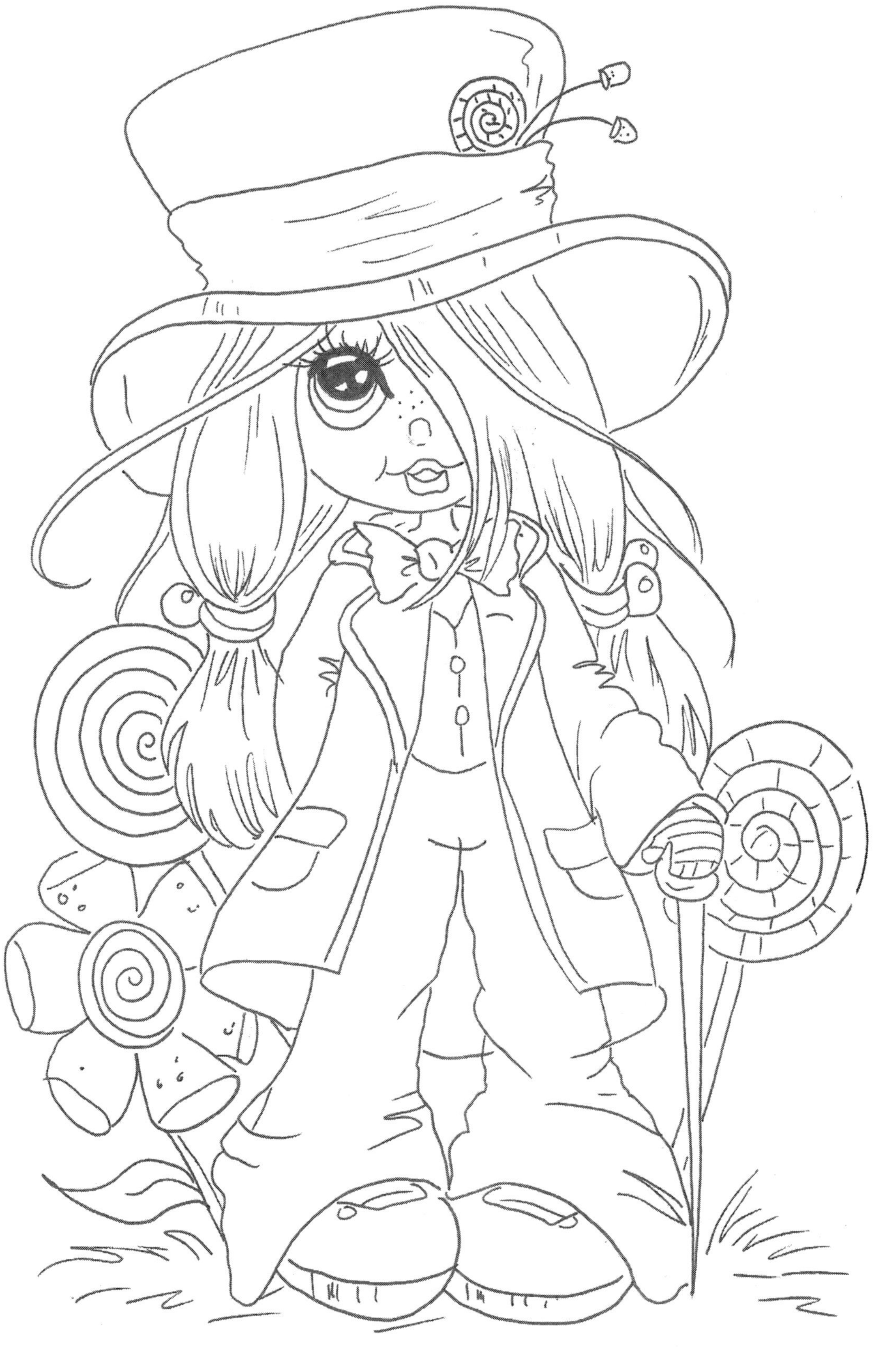

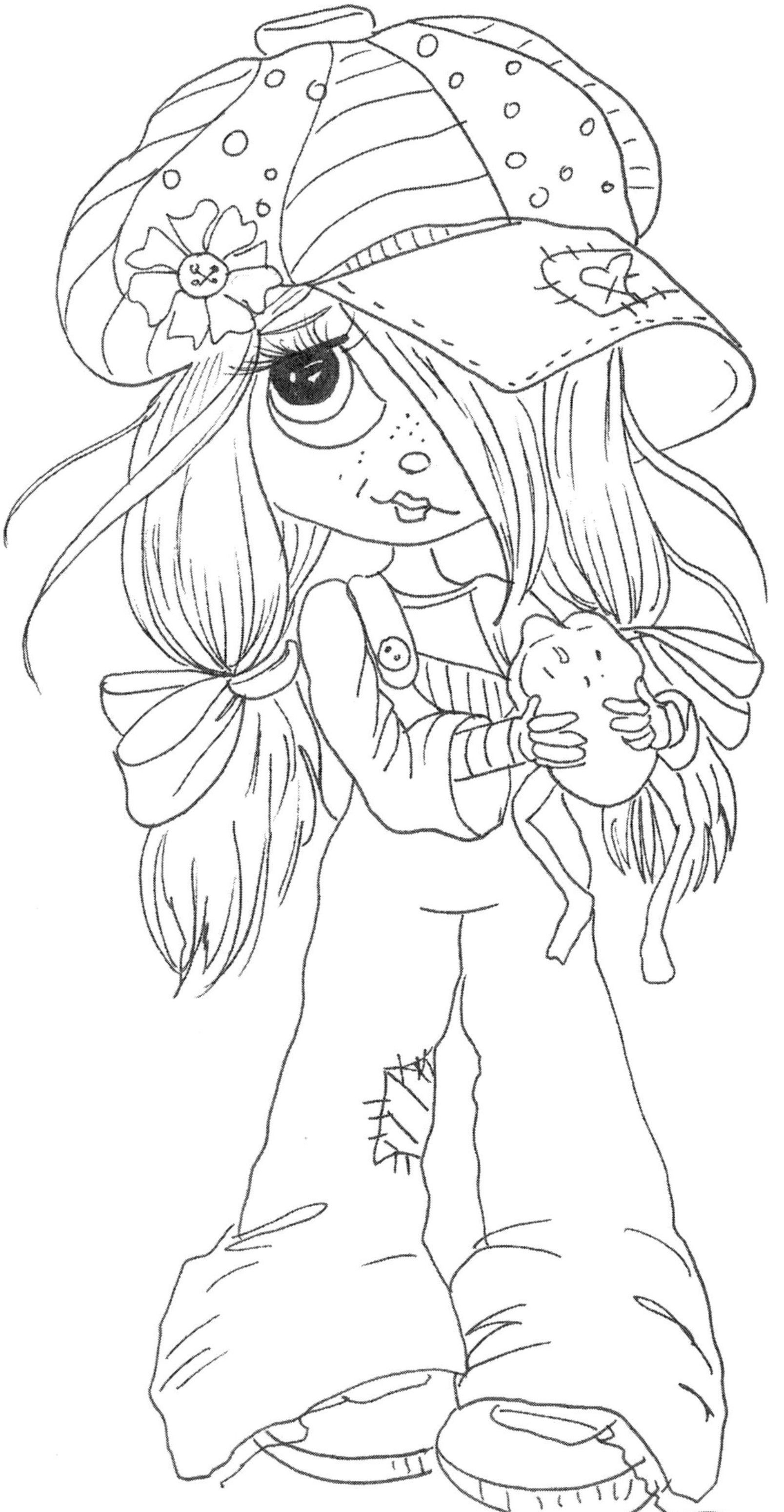

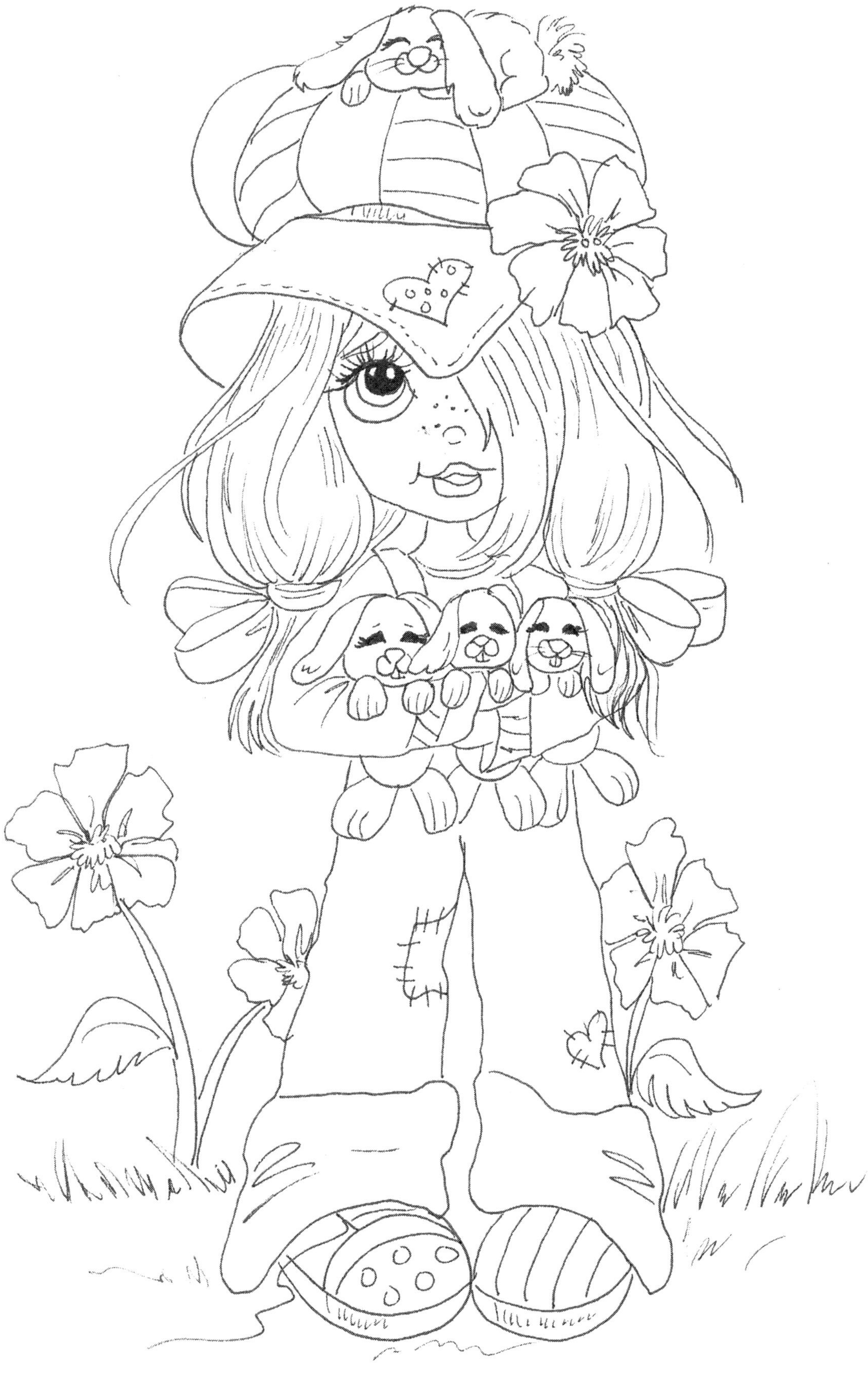

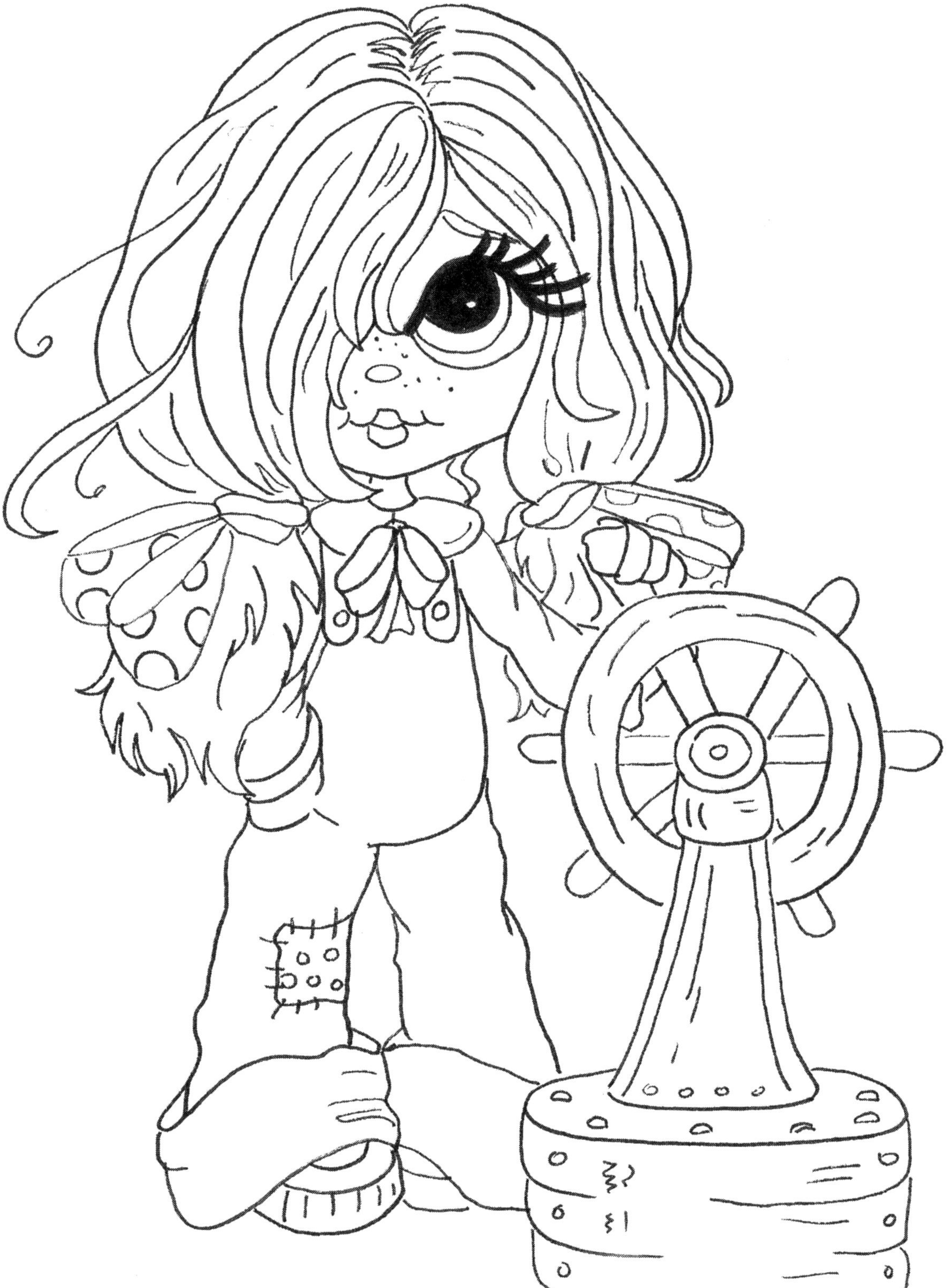

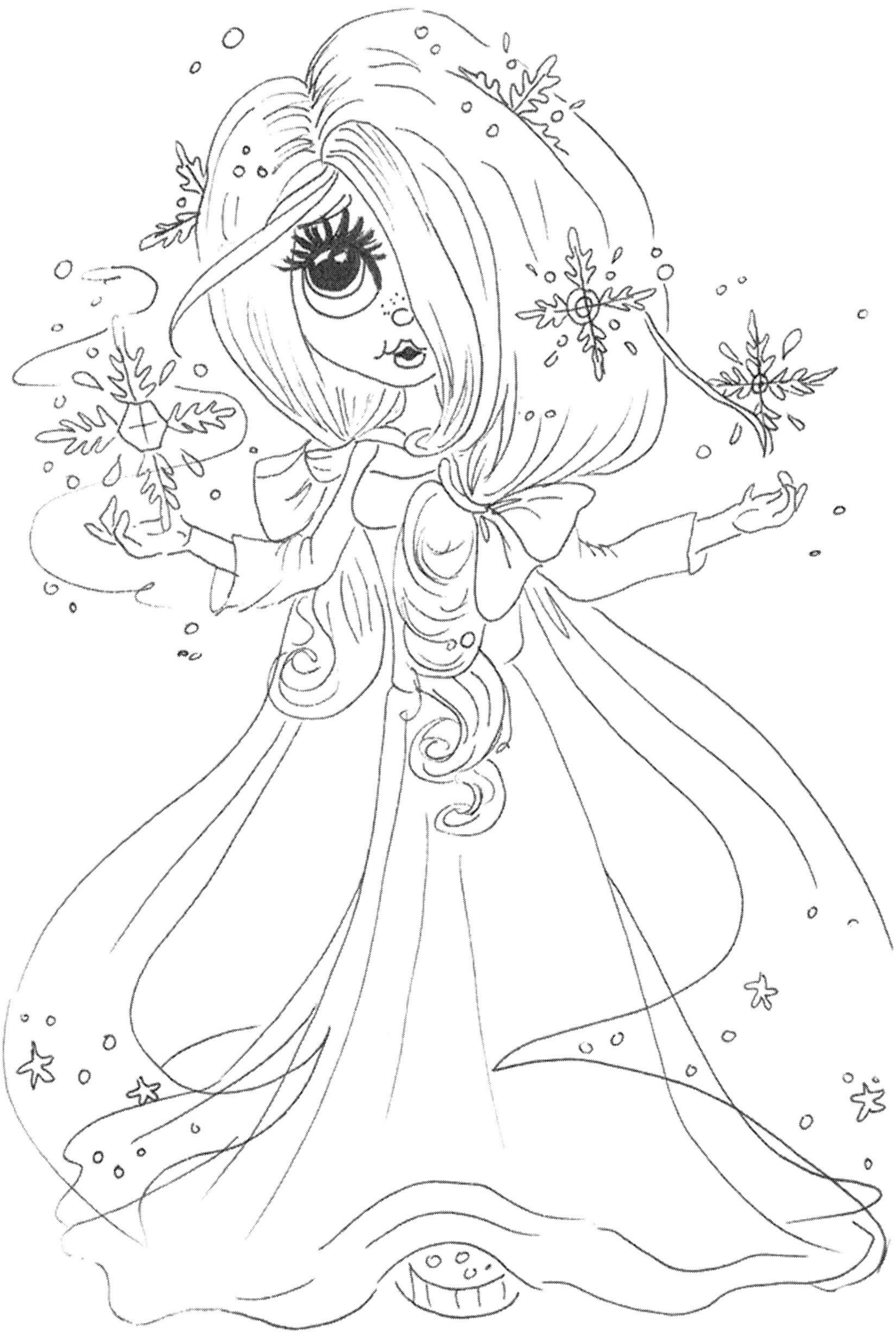

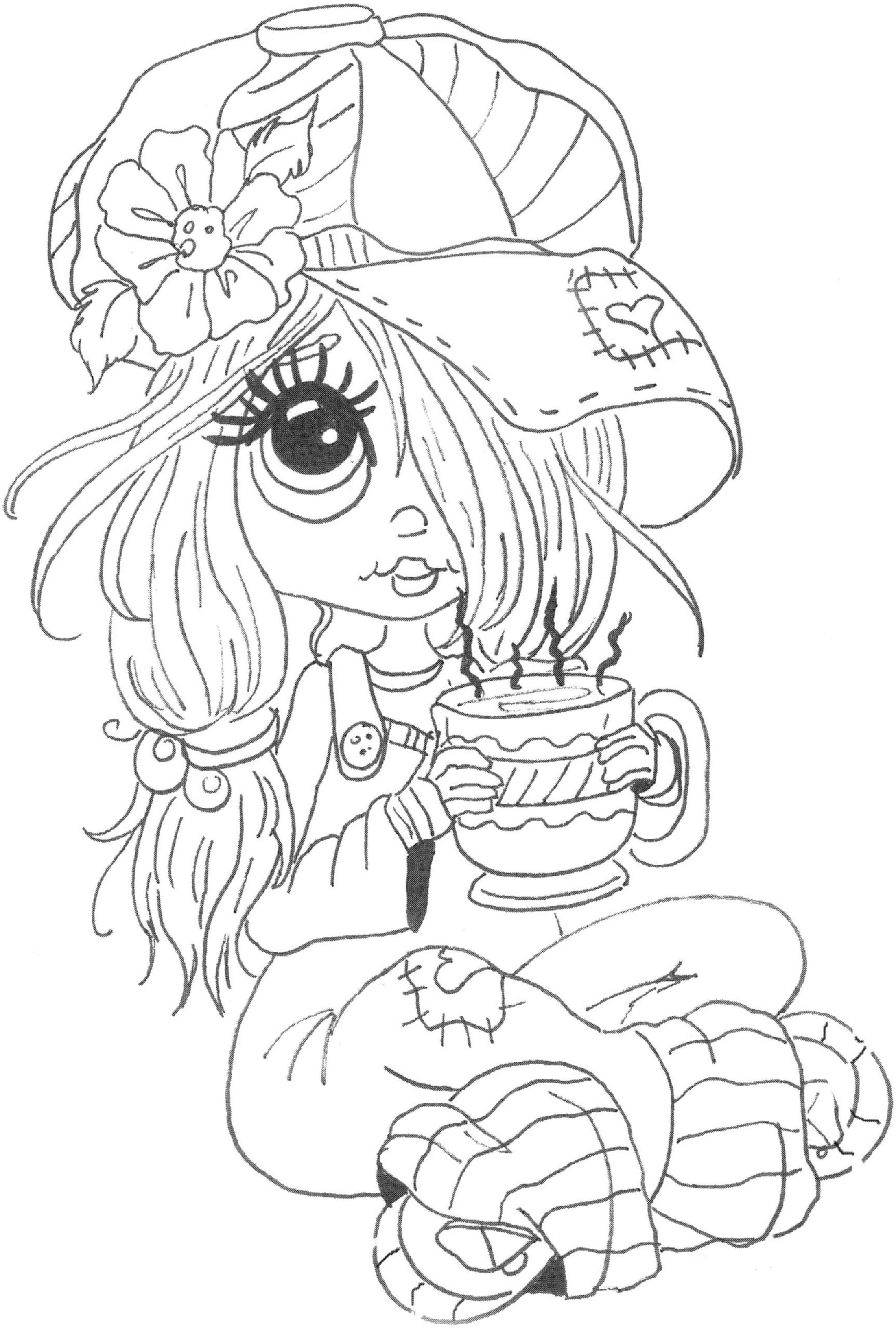

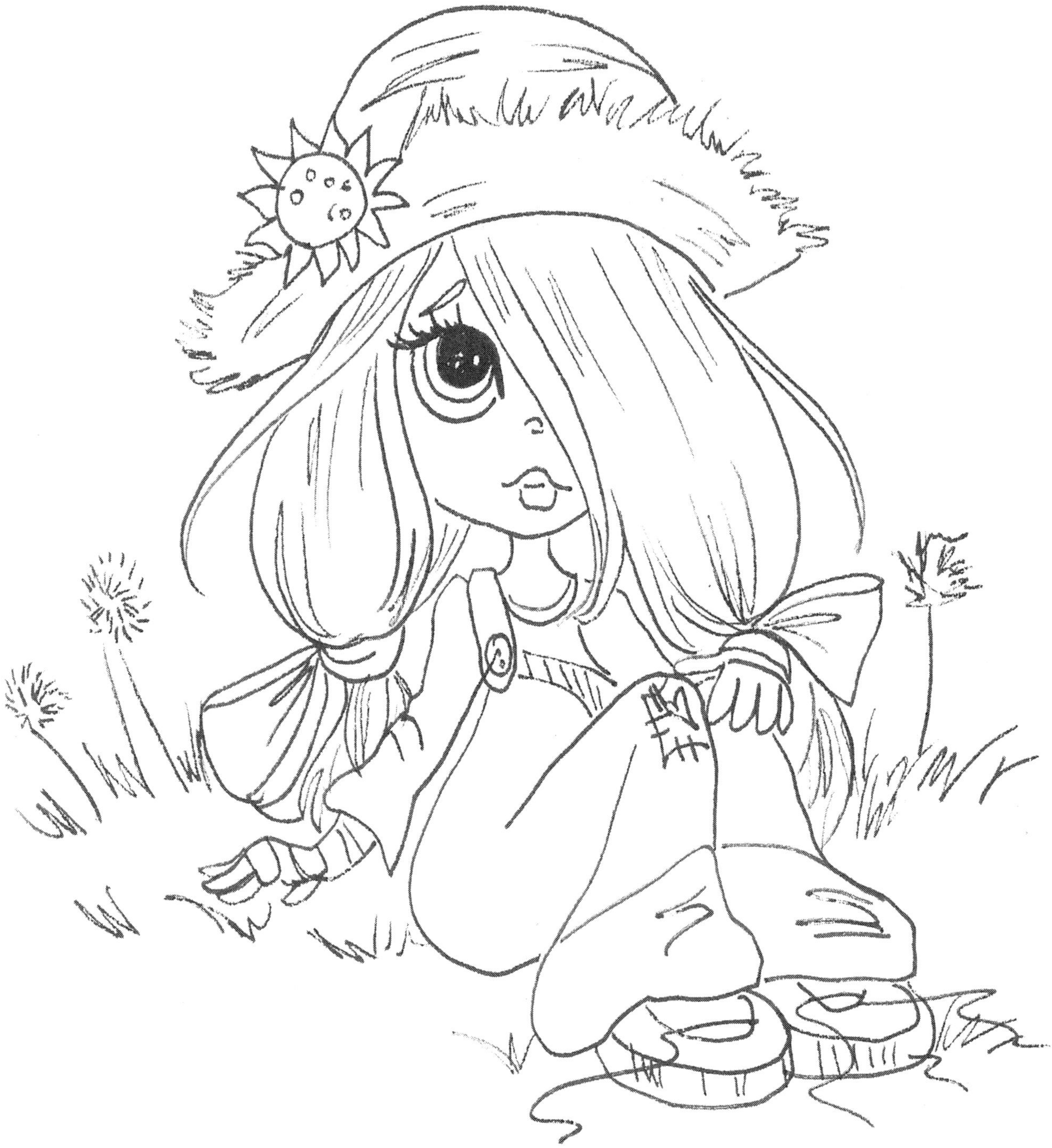

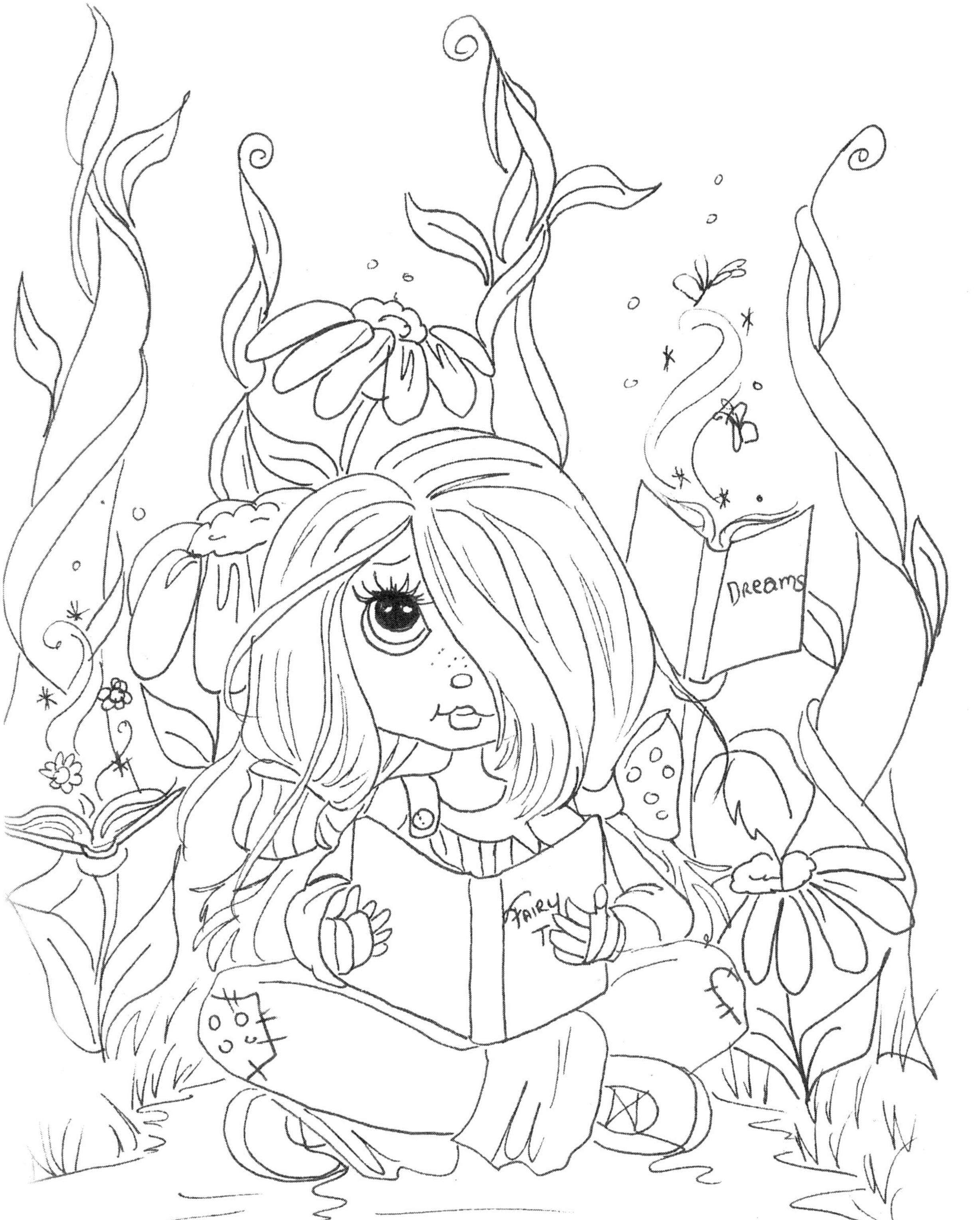
Dreams
FAIRY
T